Bible Puzzles & Fascinating Facts

The BIG FUN variety collection of crosswords, quizzes & challenges

Inspired by Faith

Bible Puzzles & Fascinating Facts
ISBN 978-0-9977556-4-0

Published by Product Concept Mfg., Inc.
2175 N. Academy Circle #200, Colorado Springs, CO 80909

Written and Compiled by Patricia Mitchell and Vicki Kuyper
in association with Product Concept Mfg., Inc.

All scripture quotations are from the King James version
of the Bible unless otherwise noted.

Scriptures taken from the Holy Bible,
New International Version®, NIV®.
Copyright © 1973, 1978, 1984 by Biblica, Inc.™
Used by permission of Zondervan.
All rights reserved worldwide.
www.zondervan.com

Sayings not having a credit listed are contributed by writers
for Product Concept Mfg., Inc. or in a rare case,
the author is unknown.

Bible Puzzles & Fascinating Facts

God gave them knowledge and skill in all learning and wisdom.

Daniel 1:17

Have Fun While You Keep Your Bible Knowledge Sharp!

Here's a big, fun variety of word search puzzles, crosswords, quizzes and more – a lively way to refresh your memory of the Bible and keep you inspired. Some are easy, some are challenging; all will give you hours of puzzle-solving enjoyment!

Signs, Symbols, and Astonishing Sights

In the Bible, God appeared in many ways.
Here are just a few of them!

ACROSS

1 God spoke to him in a burning bush
4 Angel Gabriel brought God's message to this young girl
5 God inflicted 10 plagues upon this nation to reveal His power
8 Abraham and Sarah's late-in-life son
10 God spoke to him in a still, small voice
12 Confusion of languages tower
13 Event that proved Jesus' victory over death
17 God put a star in the sky to lead them
18 Zechariah and Elizabeth's late-in-life son
19 God created this garden for Adam and Eve
20 God prepared a great fish to swallow this reluctant prophet

DOWN

2 Lot's wife turned into a pillar of __
3 God gave him the power to interpret the handwriting on the wall
6 Jesus walked on the water on this sea
7 Holy Spirit appeared as this at Jesus' baptism
9 God gave him the power to defeat Goliath
11 God gave him the power to crumble Jericho's walls
14 God told him to build an ark to survive the Flood
15 Holy Spirit appeared as tongues of __ at Pentecost
16 Along with five loaves and two of these, Jesus fed 5000
17 God sent this from heaven to feed the Children of Israel as they wandered in the desert

Answers are in the back of the book.

Bible Women Crossword

ACROSS

1 Early Christian teacher
5 Driven into the desert
   by 13 Across
6 Bore John, who became
   a Baptizer
10 Timothy's pious
   grandmother
13 Her name means "Princess"
15 First woman
17 Jacob's favored wife
19 She learned the secret
   of Samson's strength
20 Samuel's mom
23 Nabal's smart wife
24 Desert prophetess

DOWN

2 She stayed with 21 Down
3 Temple widow
4 Early Christian known
   for her needlework
7 Seller of purple cloth
8 Timothy's pious mother
9 Hosea's unfaithful wife
11 Solomon's mom
12 Sister of Lazarus
14 Wicked queen
16 Queen of Persia
18 She had 12 brothers
21 Orpah's mother-in-law
22 Magdalene

Answers are in the back of the book.

True or False?

Here's a fun way to test what you know about truths in the Bible.

1. T   F   There are many paths to God. (John 14:6)

2. T   F   God created everything that exists. (Hebrews 3:4)

3. T   F   Jesus has prepared a place in heaven for each one who believes in Him. (John 14:2)

4. T   F   When someone offends us, we should quickly publicize our side of the story. (Matthew 18:15 NIV)

5. T   F   God keeps a list of all the sins you have ever committed. (Psalm 130:3-4 NIV)

6. T   F   Certain people don't deserve our forgiveness. (Luke 6:37)

7. T   F   You can love God, yet not obey guidelines in the Bible that you find unreasonable or difficult to follow. (John 14:15)

8. T   F   Self-control is a result of the Holy Spirit's work in the believer. (Galatians 5:22-23 NIV)

9. T   F   If your enemy suffers, it serves him right; you don't need to lift a finger to help him. (Romans 12:20)

10. T   F   When you think about God's Word and meditate on what He says, your faith grows and strengthens. (Colossians 3:16)

11. T   F   There's no limit to what God can do. (Luke 1:37)

Answers are in the back of the book.

Words Matter

The world has enough critics, but it can always use champions who think about what other people might be going through... to listen to another person's perspective...to ask, "Can I help?" Follow the clues below by crossing off the words in the grid. Some words might be crossed off by more than one clue. When you are finished, the remaining words form a saying, reading left to right.

1. Cross off all names of colors.
2. Cross off all words that rhyme with pan.
3. Cross off all foods and beverages.
4. Cross off all words containing two sets of double letters.
5. Cross off all words that are names of flowers or trees.
6. Cross off all words that contain the word ant.

MILK	TWO	BUTTRESS	PLAN
THINGS	ROSE	ARE	GRANT
BAD	TEAL	CAN	FOR
COMMITTED	THE	PIE	PURPLE
HEART	OAK	RUNNING	PALM
UPSTAIRS	YELLOW	AND	RUNNING
PLEASANT	DOWN	AZURE	POMEGRANATE
SPAN	CORN	PEOPLE	ABBESS

Saying: _____

Answers are in the back of the book.

No Worries

Find the reading's **bolded words** in the word search puzzle.

    Health. Finances. **Relationships**. What's **happening** now. What might happen in the future. There's a lot to **worry** about, and most of us do. But God tells us not to worry, and for a very **practical reason**: so much of what worries us, we have no **power** to **affect** one way or the other! "Who of you by worrying can add a **single hour** to your life?" Jesus asked His **disciples**. "Since you can-not do this very **little thing**, why do you worry about the rest?" (Luke 12:25-26 NIV).

    The **time** we spend worrying **clouds** our **thinking** and **prevents** us from doing what's within our **control**, such as **adopting** healthy habits of **mind** and **body**; making sound **financial** decisions; **treating** others the way we want to be treated; **responding** wisely to **events** that touch our lives; leaving the future in **God's hands**. All this is **enough** to keep any of us too **busy** to worry!

    Turn what worries you over to God. He has **broad shoulders**. And then, free from the burden of worry, you just might **discover** how you can change things for the **better**.

```
T A Q Z N O S A E R L A C I T C A R P F W T
H J R T H T C V G F H A H E A L T H C K R Q
G Q R Y S E V R E W O P U M P J T E L E W C
U G L R Z G N I N E P P A H U J F R A Y D K
O N X N E A Q T S P E D T M I K U T Q K Z C
N I J N P S A V C R F Y G T Q A I H F T J R
E K L L G P M L A E U Z U I N I I W L P C
L N W I M O H O W S B D Z P G M H C I J O L
L I O T D W E Y N M P T L S F O E Y R N R R
T H R T Y W K C L D I I X U F C G F T J N E
J T R L N Y K U A A I N H M O N C R U P I T
V U Y E Y L H I F R Q N D S V H O M Y D O B
B C X T O C O F S F E G G E N L S Z S Z S A
A I R H X E E A D X C T O R H O Q D V F U V
P X H I Z C X U V C S A T M G U I M A S T X
R M U N T E H B R X O N V E L N Z T D O R M
J R Z G W S M Z T E Q F F B B L I U A W R X
S U U W J D X S J V V A E L S H O T U L B B
D O X V M H V B E N U O K F A L S A P F E F
N H V W W O D P P L C L C W C I K C R O Z R
A E H D L G U F C V P W Z S T V C O X P D R
H L P R E V E N T S H I R J I O D N M A C A
S G F U Z D P W Q C A M C P J D V K A Y D J
D N N K F A Q T T W M U L S H L N B S N I J
O I S T N E V E B F B V U A I D G U K W I H
G S T M Z X S N A U J N U G O D B I L O L F
```

Answers are in the back of the book.

"Encourage One Another..."

1 Thessalonians 5:11 NIV

You'll discover some encouraging words in this puzzle!

ACROSS

1 You might open a new one
4 Fury
8 President Coolidge, to friends
11 Respect
12 "Rock of __," traditional hymn
13 Cab
14 He fled from Sodom
15 Rascal
16 Goliath was one
17 Curdle
19 Mentor's student
20 Fib
21 Christmas figures
22 Native Alaskan
25 Down in the dumps
26 Lout
29 Affection
30 Elation
31 Wedding month
32 "Info forthcoming," for short
33 Prom rental, for short
34 Invigorating.
Also descriptive of a lemon.
35 Yearn, with "for"
37 Letters in distress
38 Have faith in
40 Satisfied
44 Fervor

45 Asian garment
46 Johannesburg lander
47 Choir section
48 Accessible
49 Pipe type, for short
50 Seed bread
51 Floating ice
52 Fisherman's need

DOWN

1 Baby powder
2 Gone without permission, for short
3 Computer program test version
4 Hare
5 Come to an understanding
6 Wheel cog
7 PST is three hours earlier than this
8 Wary
9 Shaft
10 Feel good about
13 Petty criminal
18 Unhappy
19 Little bit
21 Permission word
22 Keyboard key
23 Toss
24 Assess
25 Ball team, for short
27 Picnic visitor

DOWN CON'T

28 Town in Switzerland
30 Container
31 Prank
33 Explosive letters
34 Defining districts
36 Scandinavian capital
37 More angry

38 Former Russian ruler
39 Depend
40 Canaveral or Cod, for example
41 Athlete's network
42 Church section
43 Thoughtfulness
45 Cry

Answers are in the back of the book.

Transformations

Change isn't always easy, But remember this: God never changes. His love is the same yesterday, today, and forever!

Change the first word into the second word of each pair by replacing only one letter at a time. Do not scramble letter order; use only common English words, and no capitalized words.

Example:
LOSE, lone, line, fine, FIND

1. TINY

   _____
   _____
   _____
   _____
   _____

   VAST

2. POOR

   _____
   _____
   _____
   _____

   RICH

3. LESS

   _____
   _____
   _____
   _____
   _____

   MORE

4. MEAN

   _____
   _____
   _____
   _____

   KIND

5. HOLD

   _____
   _____
   _____
   _____
   _____

   GIVE

Answers are in the back of the book.

Missions Accomplished

Match the name of the Bible leader in the first column with the event in the second column.

1. David

2. Abraham

3. Deborah

4. Paul

5. Ananias

6. Esther

7. Moses

8. Joseph

9. John

10. Jonah

A. Led an army against the fearsome Canaanites and defeated them.

B. Demanded that Pharaoh let God's people leave Egypt.

C. Lived in the desert and preached repentance to the people.

D. Took on a hardened warrior, though a youth and armed only with a stone.

E. Sent by God to preach repentance to the Ninevites, even though he was reluctant to do so.

F. Endured imprisonment and floggings, yet continued to preach the Gospel message.

G. Married his pregnant fiancée because God told him in a dream that she would give birth to Jesus.

H. Uprooted his household and set out for a land promised to him by God.

I. Approached a known persecutor of the early church because God told him to do so.

J. Risked her life to save her people from a genocidal plot.

Answers are in the back of the book.

Timely Matters

All the answers in this puzzle are related to time.

ACROSS

3 Timeless

5 "One day is with the Lord as a thousand __..." (2 Peter 3:8)

9 "Teach us to __ our days" (Psa. 90:12)

11 "Time is __," says the starter

13 "Time is __," says the boss

16 __ Saving Time

17 "Time __," says the harried one

18 Calendar heading

DOWN

1 "In __ time," says the procrastinator

2 "A time of war, a time of __" (Eccl. 3:8)

4 "Time and __ wait for no man"

6 "It's __ time!" sighs the impatient one

7 "A time to every __ under the heaven" (Eccl. 3:1)

8 "Time and __ happeneth to them all" (Eccl. 9:11)

10 "The Lord will deliver him in time of __" (Psa. 41:1)

12 "Time heals all __"

14 "Time is too __," says the busy one

15 Time keeper

Answers are in the back of the book.

19

Big Puzzler

People and places of the Bible are in this crossword puzzle!

ACROSS

1 Trims
6 Go quickly
10 Snow skidder
14 "Come unto me, all ye that... are heavy __" (Matt. 11:28)
15 Patmos, for example
16 Eastern church altar area
17 Dramatic production song
18 Decorative needle case
19 Deliver us from __
20 Some ark pairs
22 Henhouse gatherings
24 Old Testament priest
25 Colder
27 Cozy and comfortable
29 Old Testament patriarch
32 Couple
33 Shout of disapproval
34 Sinai leader
37 Eve's Husband
41 Writer Bombeck
43 Child
44 Infant in Paris
45 Ogle
46 Bethlehem Baby
48 Body builder's pride, for short
49 Self
51 Old Testament judge
54 Son of 29 Across
56 Prison
57 School org.
58 Speak with trilled "r"
60 Sawmill's product
64 "__ of milk and honey"

66 You have two when you tie your shoe
68 Gaelic name meaning white or fair
69 Bread spread
70 In addition
71 Monies
72 Old Testament King Hiram's city
73 "Spirit of the Lord shall __ upon him" (Isa. 11:2)
74 Destroy

DOWN

1 Messy one
2 Neck part
3 Thought
4 Queen Esther's realm
5 Kidnap
6 What 46 Across did on Calvary
7 Autumn flower
8 Bogus coin
9 Elevations
10 Joppa to Jerusalem dir.
11 Barrier
12 Poet Dickinson
13 Painter of melting clocks
21 "Anna and the King of __"
23 "They that __ in tears shall reap in joy" (Psa. 126:5)
26 Express feelings
28 Utah biking region
29 Son of 37 Across
30 "He himself __ our sins" (1 Peter 2:24 NIV)
31 Paul's place of house arrest
35 Distress call
36 Musical practice piece

DOWN Con't

38 Letter opener
39 "We cry, __, Father" (Rom. 8:15)
40 Netting
42 Region
46 Given to joking
47 "Buy the truth, and __ it not" (Pro. 23:23)
50 Chatter
52 Cliffs
53 Metallic element

54 31 Down location
55 More reasonable
56 Calvary sight
57 Judas' plan, for example
59 a character's part, as for 17 across
61 __ fide
62 Ceases
63 Impulsive
65 Fawn's mom
67 Urn

Answers are in the back of the book.

Decode the Quote

Fill in the words that match their definitions. Then, complete the solution by placing each letter that corresponds with its matching number into the spaces below. When you're finished, you'll find what president ABRAHAM LINCOLN had to say about prayer.

Skin

___ ___ ___ ___ ___ ___
8   5   9   10   1   13

Scowl

___ ___ ___ ___ ___ ___
18   17   14   16   5   9

Bulb blossom

___ ___ ___ ___ ___
12   20   17   1   21

Convoy

__ __ __ __ __ __ __
19   3   9   3   4   3   7

Schmooze

__ __ __ __ __ __
2   14   6   7   14   6

What an eggwhite omelet lacks

__ __ __ __
11   14   17   15

1		2	3	4	5		6	5	5	7		8	9	1	4	5	7			
10	3	7	11		12	1	10	5	13		12	14		10	11			—		
15	7	5	5	13		6	11		12	2	5		14	4	5	9				
16	2	5	17	10	1	7	18		19	14	7	4	1	19	12	1	14	7		
12	2	3	12		1		2	3	8		3	6	13	14	17	20	12	5	17	11
7	14		14	12	2	5	9		21	17	3	19	5		12	14		18	14	.

Answers are in the back of the book.

Rhyme Time

Each clue can be answered with two rhyming words. All refer to a well-known Bible figure, and the spaces show how many letters are in the answer. Example:

Adam's son's great canines = **C A I N ' S   D A N E S**

1. First woman's wheat bundles

— — — — ,   — — — — — — —

2. Gospel writer's English noblemen

— — — — — ,   — — — — —

3. Ark builder's feathery scarves

— — — — — — ,   — — — —

4. Naomi's faithful daughter-in-law's small enclosures

— — — — — ,   — — — — — — —

5. Moses' brother's long-legged wading birds

— — — — — — ,   — — — — — — —

6. Gospel writer's green spaces

— — — — — ,   — — — — — —

7. Epistle writer's fairground shelters

— — — — — ,   — — — — — — —

8. The Baptizer's young deer

— — — — — ,   — — — — — —

Answers are in the back of the book.

All in the Family

Get acquainted with these Bible families! Match the description in the first column with the family member in the second column.

1. Jesus often visited the Bethany home of Mary and Martha and their brother.

2. This beloved son of King David connived to take his father's throne.

3. Jesus healed this disciple's mother-in-law's fever.

4. In the very first family, this son murdered his brother, Abel.

5. Their jealousy led his eleven brothers to sell him into slavery.

6. Leaving their father Zebedee's fishing business, James and his brother went to follow Jesus.

7. King David's son with Bathsheba was renowned for his wisdom and wealth.

8. This missionary followed his mother Eunice and grandmother Lois in the faith.

9. Abraham's wife bore a son, Isaac, late in life.

10. This faithful daughter-in-law left her own land to go with her widowed mother-in-law, Naomi.

11. His brother Aaron spoke for him in front of Pharaoh of Egypt.

A. Peter

B. John

C. Ruth

D. Solomon

E. Sarah

F. Cain

G. Moses

H. Joseph

I. Timothy

J. Lazarus

K. Absalom

Answers are in the back of the book.

Funny Money

Our view of money reflects our relationship with God and those around us. God promises, "Seek first his kingdom and his righteousness, and all these things will be given to you as well." (Matthew 6:33 NIV).
See if you know the answer to these money questions!

1. According to records, who guarded the first U.S. Mint in Philadelphia?
   a. Watchdog b. 2 Soldiers c. It wasn't guarded

2. If you stack 48 pennies, how high would your stack be?
   a. 1" b. 2" c. 3"

3. About how much was the price of a gallon of gas in 1950?
   a. 10¢ b. 20¢ c. 30¢

4. The first non-mythical person to appear on a regular-issue U.S. coin was President Lincoln in 1909. Who was the first non-mythical woman to appear?
   a. Martha Washington
   b. Susan B. Anthony
   c. Queen Isabella of Spain

5. What dollar denomination is a Benjamin?
   a. $50 b. $100 c. $500

6. Approximately how much does the average American spend on fast food annually?
   a. $1,000 b. $3,000 c. $5,000

7. What percent of income is a literal tithe?
   a. 5% b. 10% c. 15%

8. During which war did the United States first start printing bills?
   a. Revolutionary War
   b. Spanish-American War
   c. Civil War

9. How much does it cost to produce a nickel?
   a. Less than it costs to produce a dime
   b. More than it costs to produce a dime
   c. About the same as it costs to produce a dime

10. About how long does a dollar bill last in circulation?
    a. Less than 6 years
    b. More than 10 years
    c. Only one year

Answers are in the back of the book.

Flower Show

He hath made every thing beautiful in his time.

Ecclesiastes 3:11

Unscramble the letters for a list of favorite flowers. Then unscramble the letters in parenthesis for another colorful flower, and you'll have a full bouquet!

1. A A T N O N R C I

__ __ __ __ __ __ (__) __ __

2. L F D F D O A I

__ (__) __ __ __ __ __ __

3. S O G L U I D L A

__ __ __ (__) __ __ __ __ __

4. P A A G R O D N S N

(__) __ __ __ __ __ __ __ __ __

5. S A N Y P   __ __ __ (__) __

6. Z L E A A A   __ __ __ __ (__) __

7. H D I A A L   __ __ __ __ (__) __

Answer: __ __ __ __ __ __ __

Answers are in the back of the book.

Prayer Power

Many of the words in this puzzle are related to prayer.

ACROSS

1 Truth
5 Prep school (Abbr.)
9 Uninvolved
11 "Thy will be ___" (Matt. 6:10)
12 Child-bearer
13 Avant-garde art movement
14 Joppa to Jerusalem dir.
15 Computer memory unit
17 Commandments number
18 Tan colors
20 How Solomon judged
22 Sect.
23 Providence locale (Abbr.)
24 Early patriot's descendent, perhaps
27 "Deliver us from __" (Matt. 6:13)
29 "Make a joyful __ unto the Lord" (Psa. 100:1)
31 4-wheeler
32 "Ask, and it shall be __ you" (Matt. 7:7)
33 Org.
34 "__ us not into temptation" (Matt. 6:13)

DOWN

1 Renown
2 "__! and Did My Savior Bleed?" hymn title
3 "Thy kingdom __" (Matt. 6:10)
4 Cat
5 Total
6 Raccoon-like animal
7 South American mountain range
8 College head
10 "Our __," prayer opening (Matt. 6:9)
16 Making bundles of hay
18 Topeka locale (Abbr.)
19 Paducah locale (Abbr.)
20 Leah and Rachel to Jacob
21 Crawling vines
22 __ vu
24 Swimming pool jump
25 Not ashore
26 "A time to __, and a time to sew" (Eccl. 3:7)
28 Hosp. staffer
30 "Thou anointest my head with __" (Psa. 23:5)

It All Adds Up!

Find the word each of the three clues have in common. Write it in the blank to the right. These three solutions form a fourth vertical puzzle. The numbers indicate the number of letters in each solution word. The + tells you the word's position.

For example: + **mate**, + **food** and **lost** + is **SOUL**.

mast +   (4)   _____ +
+ quarters
+ phones

thresh +   (4)   + _____
+ up
with +

lunch +   (3)   + _____
chatter +
boom +

Final Answer: (5)   _____

Hint: 2 Corinthians 12:10

Answers are in the back of the book.

Good Words

Words of encouragment and self-forgiveness go a long way toward freeing you from feelings of shame and inferiority. Pick the definition that best fits the "good word".

1. **EFFERVESCENT**
a. Kind
b. Lively
c. Nice

2. **INTREPID**
a. Courageous
b. Gentle
c. Agreeable

3. **ESTEEMED**
a. Essential
b. Honored
c. Nurturing

4. **ETHICAL**
a. Enthusiastic
b. Secure
c. Principled

5. **COMMENDABLE**
a. Worthy
b. Intelligent
c. Poised

6. **PROLIFIC**
a. Productive
b. Friendly
c. Clean

7. **EMPATHETIC**
a. Powerful
b. Zealous
c. Understanding

8. **HUMANITARIAN**
a. Compassionate
b. Fun
c. Popular

9. **CONTEMPLATIVE**
a. Contented
b. Reflective
c. Graceful

10. **MUNIFICENT**
a. Distinguished
b. Generous
c. Lucid

Answers are in the back of the book.

Abundance Abounds

Your God is a God of huge harvest.

Here's a puzzle designed around the theme of abundance.

ACROSS

1 Significant
3 Outstanding; awesome
9 Big-hearted
11 Hope for
12 Limitless
14 Crop
16 Riches
17 Bestow
20 __-of-the-crop
21 "He which soweth bountifully shall __ also bountifully" (2 Cor. 9:6)
22 Big
23 Satisfied
25 Ask God
27 Awe-struck
28 Gives aid to
29 Present

DOWN

2 "My cup runneth __" (Psa. 23:5)
4 Surpass
5 Lush; abundant
6 "Ask what I shall __ thee" (1 Kings 3:5)
7 Ample
8 Advantages
10 Bring to
11 Continual
13 "There shall be __ of blessing" (Eze. 34:26)
15 Choicest
17 Unearned mercy
18 Show favor to
19 Lots
24 Most pleasant
26 Reap

Answers are in the back of the book.

Happy Discoveries

Take delight in the Lord, and he will give you the desires of your heart.
Psalm 37:4 NIV

Put the answer to Clue 1 in box 1. Scramble the letters and drop one letter to answer Clue 2. Write the word in box 2 and the dropped letter in the left-hand box. Scramble the letters and drop one letter to answer Clue 3. Write the word in box 3 and the dropped letter in the right-hand box. Complete each row the same way, starting with a new word. When you're finished, you'll discover two new words reading vertically on both sides of the puzzle. The first line is already done for you.

1. Bed needs
2. Not those
3. KJV pronoun
4. Small field rodent
5. A few
6. Fruct- or gluc- ending
7. Ankle ailment, maybe
8. Couples

9. Box
10. Citrus
11. Yard burrower
12. One of the Three Stooges
13. Weepy
14. Price
15. Pothole filler

S	1. sheets	2. these	3. thee	S
	4.	5.	6.	
	7.	8.	9.	
	10.	11.	12.	
	13.	14.	15.	

Answers are in the back of the book.

Active Contentment

Many words are spelled the same, but have different meanings, and sometimes different pronunciations. In each sentence below, replace the bolded words with one word. Example:

Her manager was **satisfied** with the **substance** of her report.
Answer: **content**

1. It was a **pleasant** day until he got a **ticket** for speeding.
   Answer: _____

2. He's the **only one** who had to repair the **bottom** of his shoe.
   Answer: _____

3. She didn't feel **fit** when she looked into the **mineshaft**, so the event didn't go **satisfactorily**.
   Answer: _____

4. "It's only **just**," she said as we walked around the arts and crafts **show**.
   Answer: _____

5. I saw her **curtsy** on the **front** of the ship.
   Answer: _____

6. Do you have a **clue** about the group that he **facilitated**?
   Answer: _____

7. Some of the coffee I **milled** spilled all over the **lawn**.
   Answer:_____

8. It was on the **edge** of her tongue to say we should leave a more generous **gratuity**.
   Answer:_____

9. Who wants to **abandon** the group in the Mohave **sands**?
   Answer: _____

10. Despite the cold **breeze**, I continued to **meander** around the garden and **coil** the hose.
    Answer:_____

11. He **stood up** from his chair and gave her a red **flower**.
    Answer: _____

Answers are in the back of the book.

Attention!

Being aware...seeing...hearing...bring new dimensions to a routine, ordinary day. Many clues in this puzzle are designed to get your attention!

ACROSS
1 Hand holder
4 Couple
5 Some time back
6 Time piece
9 Loch __ monster
13 Vase
14 Affirmative
15 High schooler
17 Desire
18 "Three persons, __ God"
20 Promise
21 "Our Father who __ in heaven"

DOWN
1 Esther's month
2 Floor covering
3 Night light
6 Shelter
7 Miner's goal
8 French number
10 View
11 Notice
12 Downhearted
16 Shining star
17 Salamander
19 Neither's partner

Weather Forecast

Match the biblical weather event with the person or place involved.

1. There was a storm on the Sea of Galilee...

2. The sun turned dark...

3. It rained 40 days and nights...

4. A windstorm brought tongues of fire...

5. A windstorm brought a plague of locusts...

6. A great wind tore mountains and shattered rocks...

7. An earthquake dislodged a great stone...

8. Hot sun and wind withered a shady plant...

a. ...and the Holy Spirit descended upon the disciples.

b. ...but Noah and his family were safe in the ark.

c. ...but Pharaoh would not let the children of Israel leave Egypt.

d. ...but the Lord was not in it, but in a still, small voice.

e. ...and Jonah was angry with God because of his discomfort.

f. ...and the disciples saw Jesus walk on water.

g. ...and women found not Jesus, but an empty tomb.

h. ...and Jesus died.

Answers are in the back of the book.

Games We Play

I have finished the race, I have kept the faith.
2 Timothy 4:7 NIV

Challenge yourself to pick the right answer for these sports-related questions!

1. In which sport would you hear the terms "stalefish" and "mule kick" used?
   a. Skiing
   b. Swimming
   c. Snowboarding

2. Where was Super Bowl I played?
   a. Los Angeles, California
   b. Atlanta, Georgia
   c. Green Bay, Wisconsin

3. What is the maximum amount of time a golfer can look for a lost ball?
   a. 2 min. b. 3 min.
   c. 5 min.

4. In 1994, why was there no baseball World Series?
   a. Players were on strike
   b. Coaches were on strike
   c. Hot dog vendors were on strike

5. Which sport did George Washington play with his troops?
   a. Kickball
   b. Soccer
   c. Cricket

6. When was the Indianapolis Motor Speedway for car racing built?
   a. 1909 b. 1929 c. 1939

7. In the modern Olympic games, when were women first admitted as athletes?
   a. 1886 b. 1900 c. 1904

8. When was the first Wimbledon tennis tournament held?
   a. 1802 b. 1877 c. 1905

Answers are in the back of the book.

Big Puzzler

This puzzle is full of sports-related words!

ACROSS

1 Nebraska city
6 Camper's bed
9 Internist's org. (Abbr.)
12 Intense light beam
13 Cheerleader's cry
14 Caustic substance
15 Moral principles
16 Sin
17 Fall mo. (Abbr.)
18 Present
20 Plant reproductive structure
22 Diamond figure
25 More subtly ridiculing
26 Put together
27 Tennis need
29 Stir
31 Billiards player's need
32 First letter of the Arabic alphabet
36 Remain loyal (2 wds.)
39 Whiz
40 Black belt wearer's study
43 Scratched
45 Horse sound
46 Fan sound
47 Steamer's initials
48 Climate watchdog group (Abbr.)
50 Blood carriers
54 Caviar
55 Team sports figure, for short
56 Listlessness
57 Hosp. staffer
58 What the benched player did
59 Raves partner

DOWN

1 Stadium cry
2 Exerciser's need, perhaps
3 Tree type
4 Robbery
5 Bow and arrow user
6 Sailing team
7 Canoe propeller
8 King's chair
9 Aurally discernable
10 Two-wheeler, for short
11 Christ's disciple
19 Prophet of ancient times
21 Brief autobiographical sketch
22 Cave flyer
23 Hoopla
24 Football goals (Abbr.)
25 Draw
28 What a cow chews
30 Thick carpet
33 Rule

DOWN CON'T

34 Winter hazard
35 Nourished
37 Not us
38 "__ Twist," Dickens title
40 Projecting ridge
41 Fable writer
42 "He is __!" Easter proclamation (Matt. 28:6)

44 Athletic field
46 Blow
49 Legume
51 Hotel
52 Almond, e.g.
53 Sibling, for short

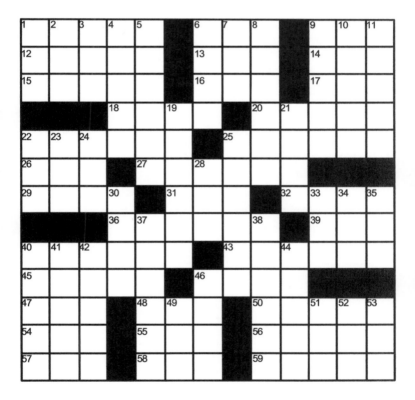

Answers are in the back of the book.

Solutions

All problems, even the toughest you face, have one good thing in common – each is an invitation to grow more...pray more...and lean more on God. Unscramble the following solution-focused words, and when you are finished, unscramble the letters in parenthesis for another important point.

1. K H N I T   L L R Y E C A

__ __ __ __ __   __ __ __ (__) __ __ __

2. E S E R A R H C

(__) __ __ __ __ __ __ __

3. O T I C J V B I T Y E

__ __ __ __ __ __ __ __ __ __ (__)

4. R S N T E N D C I M E

__ __ __ __ (__) __ __ __ __ __ __

5. R O T O   U S E C A

(__) __ __ __   __ __ __ __ __

6. N N N L G P A I

(__) __ __ __ __ __ __ __

Solution: __ __ __ __ __ __

Answers are in the back of the book.

Awesome People

Match these Bible people with their actions of compassion and faith.

1. She showed compassion and commitment to her mother-in-law, Naomi, by leaving her own land to follow Naomi to Bethlehem.

   a. Joseph

2. He readily forgave his brothers for having sold him into slavery when he was a youth.

   b. David

3. She demonstrated faith by believing the angel Gabriel's message that she would bear the Son of God.

   c. Paul

4. Despite a shipwreck, imprisonment, and other hardships, he persevered in spreading the Gospel message.

   d. Jesus

5. He obeyed God's command to prepare for a great flood, even though there was no rain in sight.

   e. Esther

6. She risked her own life to appear before the Persian king unbidden and implement a plan to save her people from Haman's wicked plot.

   f. Lydia

7. Once his great sin was pointed out to him, he turned to God in heartfelt penitence.

   g. Ruth

8. She provided generous hospitality to the missionaries who brought her the Gospel message.

   h. Noah

9. He made the ultimate sacrifice in atonement for the sins of the world.

   I. Mary

Answers are in the back of the book.

Very Funny!

Humor that is kindly and well-intentioned, friendly and lighthearted, defuses tension, lifts moods, and encourages us to see the bright side. Each answer in this puzzle relates to the theme of laughter.

ACROSS

2 "In a good __"
6 Radiant
8 Laughter
10 Circus comic
11 Gain pleasure from
16 Make glad (2 words)
17 "Happy as a __"
18 "On cloud __"
19 Entertain
21 Jubilant
22 Face of laughter
24 Joke
26 Smile maker
27 "Look on the __ side"
28 Good disposition
29 "Happy as a __ bug"

DOWN

1 Cleverly funny
3 Glee
4 "__ on air"
5 "__ pink"
7 "A __ heart hath a continual feast" (Prov. 15:15)
9 "On top of the __"
10 Quiet laughter
12 Great pleasure
13 Take part in recreation
14 "In seventh __"
15 Smile broadly
17 Some TV shows
20 Positive
23 Paradise
25 Positive expectation
26 Agreement

Answers are in the back of the book.

Biblically Named Locals Word Search

One of the oldest churches in America, is the First Church in Salem, MA, founded in 1629.

The places listed below are found in the Bible, as well as the good ol' U.S.A.. Search for the place names written forward, backward, horizontally, vertically and diagonally.

ANTIOCH
ARARAT
BETHANY
BETHEL
BETHESDA
BETHLEHEM
BETHPAGE
CALVARY
CANA
CANAAN
CARMEL
CORINTH
DAMASCUS
EMMAUS
EPHESUS
GALATIA
GOSHEN

HEBRON
ISRAEL
JERICHO
JERUSALEM
JORDAN RIVER
LEBANON
MOAB
MOUNT OLIVE
MOUNT ZION
NAZARETH
OPHIR
PALESTINE
PATMOS
REHOBOTH
SALEM
SHILOH
SHUSHAN
TYRE

Answers are in the back of the book.

```
T V S T T Z D D N O Z A C V G W J J K B P F
W S C P X I X G K R N P A U M Y J G J P U F
P H J A R N K W H T E M N M E H E L H T E B
B U X T J A C O I O S H A X C X P R Z G N L
P S B M E T L O W I E L O F R G R J K S A A
T H H O O I C R E A T J D B N I E V C R A J
K A N S H H S B M T J J G J O R H A J Y N O
P N H S N O I Z T N U O M N I T L P R X A I
S E S N H F U L T S T Y S C O V H R O F C I
U G I A C J S X K M T Y H N A R G N T H E Z
S A S V L N Y E L B A O C R J U B E E N V G
E P T U T E V X J A E G Y C U P E E I H F N
H H J G R S M N V C F L O B V O G T H K C C
P T Z D H E E G A N E R A R A D S E H T E B
E E G O R H B R B H I E B S L E M Z M G D H
R B K A S P M Q T N D P M T L O T J M K L P
E E S O L E W E T C W E M A A X D A B L G B
V Q G Y L A B H M O V C P B J P X K R L W D
I H C Z Y C T S E I V S J M B U L S D A F X
R T N Q O C F I L R U Z N Y B Q V E B C R L
N E K Y G I I O A C Y D U N S E Z G A X W A
A R U U Y U T N S M S T I A U R F N I R J P
D A A V Y N U A U V P U D H A S Z B D Y S R
R Z P M U Z M A R E U P V T M P R G T L T I
O A W O W A L F E X H Q D E M T H E R F B A
J N M G D C P D J T A U J B E N O N A B E L
```

It All Adds Up!

Find the word each of the three clues have in common. Write it in the blank to the right. These three solutions form a fourth vertical puzzle. The numbers indicate the number of letters in each solution word. The + tells you the word's position.

For example: + **mate**, + **food** and **lost** + is **SOUL**.

+ dog   (5)   _____ +
+ word
wrist +

+ break   (6)   _____+
black +
+ house

+ setter   (4)   _____+
out +
+ car

Final Answer: (5)   _____

Hint: God is yours.

Matching Pairs

The Golden Rule teaches us to "Do to others as you would have them do to you." (Luke 6:31 NIV). It helps if we learn empathy, the ability to see ourselves in the other person's shoes. Pick the phrase in the second column that completes the shoe- or feet-related sentence in the first column.

1. In the Upper Room, Jesus washed the feet of...

a. Moses

2. "I'm not worthy to carry His sandals," said...

b. Ruth

3. "You're standing on holy ground," said God to...

c. Proverbs

4. Those who hastily ate the first Passover, with coat and shoes on were the...

d. a certain woman who led a sinful life

5. A man would give his shoe to another to confirm a decision, according to the book of...

e. His disciples

6. "She washed My feet with her tears and dried them with her hair," said Jesus of...

f. Israelites

7. If we walk the path of life with integrity, we will walk securely, according to the book of...

g. God's Word

8. It's like a lamp to our feet, says the Psalmist of...

h. John the Baptist

Answers are in the back of the book.

Big Puzzler

This puzzle contains many foot- and shoe-related words.

ACROSS

1 Advanced deg.
4 Route
8 Exercise target, maybe
11 __ Grande River
12 Giant
13 Street sign word
14 Frequently, for short
15 Press
16 Scorch
17 Stocking choice, maybe
19 Briny
20 Southwestern Indian
21 Infant
22 Shoe color, perhaps
25 Fizzy drink
26 Dancing shoe
29 Winter shoe
30 Underdone
31 Former Italian currency
32 Note of debt
33 "__ Father"
34 Apes
35 Bone covered by 29 Across
37 "I'll be there in a __"
   (momentarily)
38 Construction beam material
40 Cobbler's material
44 Descriptor for shoes that fit, e.g.

45 Honey makers
46 To be in debt
47 Spoken
48 Time in office
49 Ocean
50 Dampen
51 __ Major (Big Dipper)
52 Make a mistake

DOWN

1 1 Across, for short
2 Audiophile's choice
3 Speckles
4 Ballet shoes
5 Concur
6 Walk at a fast clip
7 Egg layer
8 Sporting shoe
9 Ferry
10 Active
13 Wound cover
18 Ill-fitting shoes will do this
19 Deplete
21 Curtsy
22 Kimono sash
23 Cry softly
24 Pet (2 words)
25 Golfer's concern
27 __ of the Covenant

DOWN CON'T

28 Dancer's step
30 Jogger's delight
31 Garret
33 Cooking fat
34 Noxious vapor
36 Shoe part
37 Taunts
38 Skier's delight

39 Car shoe?
40 Smirk
41 Garden need
42 Vessel
43 Back
45 Heat unit

Answers are in the back of the book.

Good Words, Good Works

The theologian Martin Luther once noted that "God does not need our good works, but our neighbor does." Our good works – service to others, kindnesses, compassionate words and helpful actions – are to meet the real, pressing needs of those around us.

Determine the answers to the three clues in each set. If you answer correctly, the fourth word will work either before or after each of your answers.

Example:

    Place for canned goods = Pantry

    Fitness, wellbeing = Health

    Heavenly being = Angel

    Answer: Food

1. Exposed =

    __ __ __ __

    Beneath =

    __ __ __ __ __

    Fair, equitable =

    __ __ __ __

    A: __ __ __ __ __ __

2. Location =

    __ __ __ __ __

    Clock's data =

    __ __ __ __

    Single =

    __ __ __

    A: __ __ __

3. Heavily encumbered =

__ __ __ __ __ __ __

See to =

__ __

Winter wear =

__ __ __ __

A: __ __ __ __

4. Without charge =

__ __ __ __

Fewer =

__ __ __ __

Receiver's opposite =

__ __ __ __ __

A: __ __ __ __

5. Partner =

__ __ __ __

Me =

__ __ __ __

Employed =

__ __ __ __ __

A: __ __ __ __

6. Observing =

__ __ __ __ __ __

Resolve =

__ __ __ __

Sense =

__ __ __ __

A: __ __ __ __

7. Adhere to =

__ __ __ __

Use the car =

__ __ __ __

Slay =

__ __ __ __

A: __ __ __

8. Abdomen =

__ __ __ __ __

Cook's broth =

__ __ __ __ __

Car fuel, for short =

__ __ __

A: __ __ __ __ __ __ __

Answers are in the back of the book.

Decode the Lyrics

Fanny J. Crosby used over 100 pseudonyms as well as her real name during her prolific career as a hymn writer.

Fill-in the words that match their definitions. Then, complete the solution by placing each letter that corresponds with its matching number into the spaces below. When you're finished, you'll find the lyrics of a song that blind American hymn writer, FANNY J. CROSBY, wrote at the age of eight.

Cast your ballot

____ ____ ____ ____
19   1   5   17

Make a joyful noise

____ ____ ____ ____
16   11   15   13

Bow before God

____ ____ ____ ____ ____ ____ ____
3   1   18   8   2   11   6

Navigational float

__ __ __ __
21   9   1   7

Speak spitefully

__ __ __ __ __ __
12   4   10   11   13   15

Fish and chips favorite

__ __ __
14   1   20

1	2		3	2	4	5		4		2	4	6	6	7		8	1	9	10		11		4	12
																						,		
4	10	5	2	1	9	13	2		11		14	4	15	15	1	5		16	17	17			11	
4	12		18	17	16	1	10	19	17	20		5	2	4	5		11	15		5	2	11	16	
3	1	18	10	20		14	1	15	5	17	15	5	17	20		11		3	11	10	10		21	17

Answers are in the back of the book.

Comforting Words

Follow the clues by crossing off words in the grid. Some words might be crossed off by more than one clue. When you are finished, you will find words of comfort from Scripture, reading left to right.

1. Cross off all two-letter pronouns.

2. Cross off all words that end with the letter T.

3. Cross off all positive personal qualities.

4. Cross off any books of the Bible.

5. Cross off all words that contain two or more of the same consonants.

6. Cross off all words that start with "com."

7. Cross off all words that mean "three."

8. Cross off all names of musical instruments.

HE	WEST	I	COMFORT
AM	GRATITUDE	JOYFUL	WITH
THRICE	YOU	HORNS	ACTS
ALWAYS	KINDNESS	EVEN	UNTO
TEMPT	THE	US	GOODNESS
REVELATION	HARPS	END	TRINITY
TEST	OF	CONTENTMENT	THE
COMING	WE	CHURCH	TRUMPETS
PATIENCE	MANSION	WORLD	GET

Answers are in the back of the book.

Famous Words

Pick the speaker of each Bible quote!

1. "Am I my brother's keeper?"
   - a. Abel
   - b. Noah
   - c. Cain

2. "Thou shalt love thy neighbor as thyself."
   - a. Jesus
   - b. Luke
   - c. Mark

3. "Behold the man!"
   - a. Ananias
   - b. Pilate
   - c. Herod

4. "Behold the handmaid of the Lord; be it unto me according to thy word."
   - a. Mary
   - b. Dorcas
   - c. Sarah

5. "Blessed are the peacemakers: for they shall be called the children of God."
   - a. Paul
   - b. John
   - c. Jesus

6. "Silver and gold have I none; but such as I have give I thee."
   - a. Jesus
   - b. Peter
   - c. John

7. "If I perish, I perish."
   - a. Delilah
   - b. Deborah
   - c. Esther

Answers are in the back of the book.

Big Puzzler

You may have traveled some of the roads in this puzzle!

ACROSS

3 Pacific __ Highway, California
7 Ad exec's NYC avenue
9 __ Highway, old road from Michigan to Florida
12 Beverly Hills boutique drive
13 Town's thoroughfare
15 Banker's NYC street
17 White House avenue
20 __ Strip, L.A.-area street the locale of former TV series
21 "__ Mile," Chicago's Michigan Avenue

DOWN

1 Houston freeway with 18 lanes of traffic in parts
2 Memphis street of blues singers
4 Appalachian __, stretching from Georgia to Maine
5 Shopper's NYC avenue
6 Starry "Walk of Fame" boulevard
8 Crooked street in San Francisco
10 __ Highway, first road across the U.S.
11 NYC theater thoroughfare
14 __ Street, metaphor for financial well-being
16 New Orleans street that borders historic section
18 __ Trail, pre-railroad way through central North America (2 words)
19 __ 66, storied "Mother Road" from Los Angeles to Chicago

Answers are in the back of the book.

It All Adds Up!

The east face of the top of the Washington Monument has the words "Laus Deo," Latin for "praise be to God."

Find the word each of the three clues have in common. Write it in the blank to the right. These three solutions form a fourth vertical puzzle. The numbers indicate the number of letters in each solution word. The + tells you the word's position.

For example: + **mate**, + **food** and **lost** + is **SOUL**.

+ power   (4)   + _____
+ fully
free +

+ hound   (4)   + _____
+ cast
+ desk

+ time   (5)   + _____
+ shade
+ gown

Final Answer: (4)   _____

                       Hint: God is...

Answers are in the back of the book.

Words of Prayer

God invites us to pray for those who go through struggles, and there are many examples throughout the Bible. Match those who prayed, with the prayer each made to God.

1. Hannah

2. Abraham

3. Paul

4. Moses

5. David

6. Jesus' disciples

7. Solomon

8. Jairus

9. Prodigal son

a. This missionary prayed that God would remove an ailment he called a "thorn in the flesh."

b. He prayed to Jesus that He would restore his little daughter who had died.

c. In the temple, this distraught woman prayed for a baby, and God blessed her with a son, Samuel.

d. He prayed that God would provide a way across the Red Sea and away from pursuing Egyptians.

e. This king prayed for wisdom rather than ask for wealth and glory.

f. He prayed for forgiveness for leaving his father's house and wasting his inheritance.

g. He bargained with God in hopes that enough God-fearing people lived in Sodom to save it.

h. Fearful for their lives, they prayed during a storm on the Sea of Galilee.

i. He prayed for forgiveness for an adulterous relationship and for bringing about a murder.

Answers are in the back of the book.

Broaden Your Horizons!

*Oh that thou wouldest bless me indeed, and enlarge my coast,
and that thine hand might be with me, and that thou wouldest
keep me from evil, that it may not grieve me!
And God granted him that which he requested.
Prayer of Jabez, 1 Chronicles 4:10*

Have you ever been hesitant to apply for a job? Try out
for a team? Wonder if you can dance, sing, be happier?
Give yourself a chance to explore something new. In this
puzzle, you may discover many things you'd like to try!

ACROSS
1 Swift animals
5 Scott Joplin compositions
9 Visual
11 Zion National Park state
12 Singer's voice, maybe
13 Call
14 You might want to sail it
15 M.S. evaluator
17 Commanded
18 Lifts
20 You can strum one
22 Friend
23 Chicago's transport, for short
24 Beret
27 Exits
29 Comment on
31 Old Testament book
32 Accra's locale
33 Make reference to
34 Female 1 Across

DOWN
1 You can connect them
2 Fencer's sword
3 Gas burner
4 __ Grande
5 Join a marathon, e.g.
6 Dickens' "__ of Two Cities"
   (2 wds.)
7 Sports
8 Outbuilding, maybe
10 Invent
16 Conversation

DOWN Cont'd

18 East Coast state (Abbr.)
19 Jr.'s dad
20 Netting
21 Supreme (Prefix)
22 Verse
24 "Bye-bye"

25 Jesus' grandmother, by tradition
26 Legumes
28 __ Francisco
30 Advanced degree

Answers are in the back of the book.

It's the Thought That Counts

Our thoughts are important! The way we think affects our happiness, relationships, work...and our whole lives!

The Bible contains many thoughts about thoughts! Each verse below, however, has a missing "thought" or two. Complete the sentences with words from the box below (all words will be used once).

HONEST	THOUGHT	HEARTS	COMMIT
GIVE	THINGS	WORKS	ONE
ESTABLISHED	MEDITATE	WHICH	EVIL
FALL	THINKING	HEART	DELIGHT
NOT	VIRTUE	KNEW	WAYS
GENERATIONS	WAYS	REPORT	INTENTS
NIGHT	DISCERNER	SEARCH	TOWARD
MY	FIRM	RIGHT	ANY
WEIGHS	COUNSEL	CAREFUL	

1. My thoughts are _____ your thoughts, neither are your _____ my _____ , saith the Lord. (Isaiah 55:8)

2. Whatsoever things are true, whatsoever things are _____, whatsoever things are just, whatsoever things are pure, whatsoever things are lovely, whatsoever things are of good _____ ; if there be any _____, and if there be _____ praise, think on these things. (Philippians 4:8)

3. I know the thoughts that I think _____ you, saith the Lord, thoughts of peace, and not of _____, to _____ you an expected end. (Jeremiah 29:11)

4. The _____ of the Lord standeth forever, the thoughts of his heart to all _____ . (Psalm 33:11)

5. _____ of you with taking _____ can add to his stature _____ cubit? (Luke 12:25)

6. A person may think their own ways are _____ , but the Lord _____ the heart. (Proverbs 21:2 NIV)

7. His _____ is in the law of the Lord; and in his law doth he _____ day and _____ . (Psalm 1:2)

8. If you think you are standing _____ , be _____ that you don't _____ ! (1 Corinthians 10:12 NIV)

9. _____ me, O God, and know my _____ : try me, and know _____ thoughts. (Psalm 139:23)

10. _____ thy _____ unto the Lord, and thy thoughts shall be _____ . (Proverbs 16:3)

11. The word of God...is a _____ of the thoughts and _____ of the heart. (Hebrews 4:12)

12. Jesus _____ what they were _____ and asked, "Why are you thinking these _____ in your _____?" (Luke 5:22 NIV)

Answers are in the back of the book.

Keep What You Love

...a time to keep, and a time to cast away.
Ecclesiastes 3:6

Yes it's important to cast out the clutter in our lives. But this puzzle is full of keepers of all kinds!

ACROSS
5 You have it when you play
6 Allegiance
8 Recollections
10 Heart's emotion
11 They might be right there or online
15 Conversation with God
16 Belief in God
18 Positive outlook
21 You're wished sweet ones at night
22 It puts a bounce in your step
23 Amazement
24 They're great to recall (2 words)
25 Loveliness

DOWN
1 Worth
2 Exaltation
3 Marvel
4 Rely on
5 Household members, most often
7 Ecstasy
9 "Tickled pink" feeling
12 Grin
13 Reason, as to do something
14 Ingenuity
17 Delectation
19 Inner contentment
20 Expectation

Answers are in the back of the book.

Transformations

Faith is life-changing because God changes lives. Follow the path of these word pairs to transform them. Change the first word into the second word of each pair by replacing only one letter at a time. Do not scramble letter order, use only common English words, and no capitalized words.

Example: LOSE, lone, line, fine, FIND

1. HURT

   _____
   _____
   _____
   _____
   CALM

2. FEAR

   _____
   _____
   _____
   _____
   PRAYER

3. STAY

   _____
   _____
   _____
   _____
   FREE

4. REAL

   _____
   _____
   _____
   _____
   LIFE

5. TRUE

   _____
   _____
   _____
   _____
   LOVE

Answers are in the back of the book.

Loyal, Disloyal

Choose the correct answer to these Bible questions about loyalty – and its opposite!

1. This prince's loyalty to his friend, David, compelled him to tell David of his father's murderous intentions and make possible David's escape:
   a. Samuel
   b. Jonathan
   c. Absalom

2. This woman's disloyalty to her husband caused the downfall of one of Israel's warriors:
   a. Delilah
   b. Jezebel
   c. Gomer

3. When this young man abandoned a mission trip, he caused a rift between Paul and Barnabas:
   a. Timothy
   b. Titus
   c. John Mark

4. Her loyalty to the Israelites was affirmed when she deceived and then killed an enemy commander, Sisera:
   a. Hannah
   b. Delilah
   c. Jael

5. This mother's loyalty to God and her promise to Him was confirmed when she presented her son to Eli the priest:
   a. Sarah
   b. Hannah
   c. Mary

6. This disciple's loyalty to Jesus was severely tested, and failed, when a servant-girl asked him if he was a disciple of Jesus:
   a. Thomas
   b. John
   c. Peter

7. This disciple's loyalty to Jesus compelled him to stand at the foot of Jesus' cross:
   a. John
   b. James
   c. Matthew

8. This uncle of Esther encouraged her to remain loyal to her own people, even though it could mean death for her:
   a. Haman
   b. Ahasuerus
   c. Mordecai

Answers are in the back of the book.

Good Questions

Many men and women in the Bible were not afraid to ask for what they wanted, even when their request might have seemed impossible. Match the name in the list with the question the person asked; each name will be used only once.

GIDEON	MARTHA	JABEZ
PAUL	HEZEKIAH	ELIJAH
MOSES	THIEF ON THE CROSS	SARAH
BARTIMAEUS	REBEKAH	JAIRUS

1. He asked for someone to speak for him in front of Pharaoh, claiming a speech impediment.

2. He prayed for more time on Earth, and God added 15 years to his life.

3. He placed a wool fleece on the threshing floor and asked God for a sign that he could lead Israel to a victory; God answered his request.

4. Abraham's servant prayed that the young woman who extended hospitality to him would be the one God intended for Isaac's bride, and God caused this woman to welcome him.

5. He prayed for the removal of a disability, but God replied that His grace was sufficient for him.

6. She had given up hope of ever conceiving, and when the Lord announced that she would bare a son, she laughed.

7. She begged Jesus to come to her home quickly so He could heal her ailing brother. Jesus allowed Lazarus to die, but then increased her faith by raising him from the grave.

8. He begged Jesus to come to his home and heal his daughter, who had died; and He returned life to her.

9. This blind beggar pleaded with Jesus to restore his sight, and Jesus granted his request on account of his faith.

10. This man prayed that God would bless his work and enlarge his territory, and God did exactly that.

11. This man asked Jesus for forgiveness, and Jesus assured him that he would be with Him in paradise.

12. He prayed that God would show His sovereign power by producing flames on an altar he had built, alongside an altar the worshipers of Baal had built. God sent a consuming fire.

Answers are in the back of the book.

Big Puzzler

Relax and enjoy solving this modern day crossword puzzle!

ACROSS

1 Affirms
6 South American nation
10 Big __, London landmark
13 Limited
15 Cry of dismay
16 Paris street
17 New Testament Roman ruler
18 Ride the waves
19 Fall mo.
20 Gardener's medium
22 Fill with joy
24 Jesus, the __ Shepherd
26 Operator
28 Challenge
29 Damage
30 Happy
31 Filleted
32 Pie __ mode (2 words)
33 Swift
34 Computer Keyboard key
35 Tropical malady
37 Have
41 Movie scene
42 Canter
43 Deer cousin
44 Tent fastener
47 Winged
48 Work's opposite
49 Domicile
50 Word book (Abbr.)
51 Fastener
52 Creative products
54 Seers
56 English Title
57 River dam
59 Resurrection Day
63 Beverage
64 Zilch
65 Formal agreement
66 Query
67 Air pollution
68 Ceasefire

DOWN

1 Athletic org.
2 By way of
3 Solo
4 What Solomon had
5 Sedate
6 Dads
7 Got away from
8 Less common
9 '80s athletic org.
10 Coarse ankle-high work shoe
11 Card game
12 Got as profit

DOWN CON'T
14 Sin
21 City in Oklahoma
23 Baals
24 Big celebration
25 Spoken
27 Rested
29 Noah's son
30 Stride
31 Top-notch
33 Without cost
34 Portal
36 Crooked
37 Chatter
38 Snaky fish
39 Strike

40 Heavens
42 Nurse's trait, for short
44 Cascade mountain
45 Early American British
   supporters
46 Commuter train company
47 Japanese martial art
48 Quarterback
50 Imagine
51 Chest thumper
53 Has
55 Still
58 Cleaning cloth
60 Greek letter
61 List ender
62 Bread choice

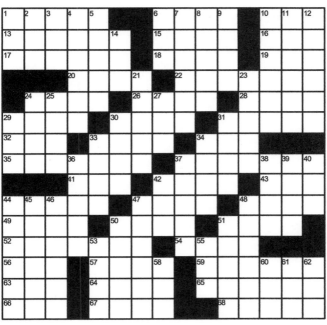

Answers are in the back of the book.

Happy Discoveries

You don't have to take a trip to see amazing sights. There are wonderful things all around us if we only open our eyes to discover them. In this puzzle, discover new words. You cannot see them without searching.

Put the answer to Clue 1 in box 1. Scramble the letters and drop one letter to answer Clue 2. Write the word in box 2 and the dropped letter in the left-hand box. Scramble the letters and drop one letter to answer Clue 3. Write the word in box 3 and the dropped letter in the right-hand box. Complete each row the same way, starting with a new word. When you're finished, you'll discover two new words reading vertically on both sides of the puzzle.

1. Clutch
2. Exchange blows
3. Knock
4. Extols
5. Church peaks

6. Iron
7. Browsed, as sheep
8. School level
9. Challenge

10. KJV "yours"
11. Slim
12. Louse
13. Glare
14. Fee per hour
15. Time period

	1.	2.	3.	
	4.	5.	6.	
	7.	8.	9.	
	10.	11.	12.	
	13.	14.	15.	

Answers are in the back of the book.

An Emotional Response

Match the Bible name in the first column with his or her feelings and response in the second column.

1. Joseph

2. Ruth

3. Paul

4. Abraham

5. Felix

6. Elijah

7. Lydia

8. Jonah

a. This Old Testament prophet was depressed because he felt that he was the only one left who believed in the true God.

b. Fear for his safety led this patriarch to present Sarah as his sister instead of his wife.

c. This Old Testament prophet became angry when God forgave the people of a wicked city rather than destroy the city.

d. His devotion to his fiancée caused him to consider quietly breaking their engagement rather than publicly shame her because of her pregnancy.

e. This governor's feeling that he could listen to the Gospel message at a later, more convenient time led him to dismiss Paul.

f. This apostle's reliance on God gave him contentment, regardless of his particular circumstances.

g. Her compassion compelled her to accompany her mother-in-law into a foreign land and see to her survival.

h. This woman from Thyatira was so happy to hear the Gospel message that she opened her home to Paul and his companions.

Answers are in the back of the book.

It's Only a Number

Choose the right answer for each question about numbers in the Bible.

1. How many books are in the King James Version of the Bible?
   a. 36 b. 66 c. 86

2. How many days did water remain on Earth including the 40 days and 40 nights of rain?
   a. 90 b. 150 c. 365

3. How many days did Jonah remain in the body of the great fish God had sent to him?
   a. 3 b. 7 c. 12

4. How many original tribes of Israel were there in the Old Testament?
   a. 10 b. 12 c. 33

5. When Jesus rose from the tomb on Easter morning, how many days did He remain on Earth?
   a. 3 b. 12 c. 40

6. How many times were the disciples to forgive others, according to Jesus?
   a. 70 x 7 b. 12 x 12 c. 144

7. How many men did Moses send to spy on the land of Canaan?
   a. 2 b. 12 c. 40

8. How many people were in the ark during the Great Flood?
   a. 8 b. 12 c. 33

9. How many years did Israel spend in exile in Babylon?
   a. 70 b. 700 c. 1,000

10. After Jesus' resurrection, how many days was it until Pentecost?
    a. 30 b. 40 c. 50

Answers are in the back of the book.

Echoes

Each clue can be answered with two rhyming words.
All refer to something of beauty, and the spaces show
how many letters are in the answer.
Example:
Compassionate mentality K I N D   M I N D

1. Squad's ray of sunshine ___ ___ ___ ___   ___ ___ ___ ___

2. Refined, beautiful area ___ ___ ___ ___ ___   ___ ___ ___ ___ ___

3. Heavenly smooch ___ ___ ___ ___ ___   ___ ___ ___ ___

4. Grin trend ___ ___ ___ ___ ___   ___ ___ ___ ___

5. Fresh outlook ___ ___ ___ ___   ___ ___ ___ ___

6. Pleasant getaway spot

___ ___ ___ ___ ___   ___ ___ ___ ___ ___ ___

7. Intelligent chest-thumper

___ ___ ___ ___ ___   ___ ___ ___ ___

8. Pious yell ___ ___ ___ ___ ___ ___   ___ ___ ___ ___

9. Pleasant glow ___ ___ ___ ___   ___ ___ ___ ___

10. Eye-twinkle connection ___ ___ ___ ___   ___ ___ ___ ___

Answers are in the back of the book.

Color Your World

Life is a mix of light and dark. God, the consummate artist, has designed a meaningful story for you. Never fear the dark, because He is there. Bask in the light, because He is there. In this crossword puzzle, you'll find many "colorful" clues!

ACROSS
1 Chew
5 Centers
9 Extremely wealthy person
11 On a cruise
12 Orange
13 Business wear
14 Oolong
15 Ouch!
17 Era
18 Breathe in
20 Unleavened breads
22 Chemist's meas.
23 Chicago transport, for short
24 Tint
27 Light brown
29 Black
31 Negatives
32 Dark gray
33 Colors
34 Walked

DOWN
1 Annoying insect
2 Label
3 "Whereby we cry, __, Father" (Rom. 8:15)
4 Trouble
5 Owns
6 Customary
7 Off-white
8 Fill
10 Yellow-brown
16 Complete items
18 Programmer's dept.
19 Like
20 "The Real __"
21 Jibe
22 Patch
24 Gray-white
25 "Come __ me, all ye that labour" (Matt. 11:28)
26 Watched
28 Ship initials
30 Deli order, for short

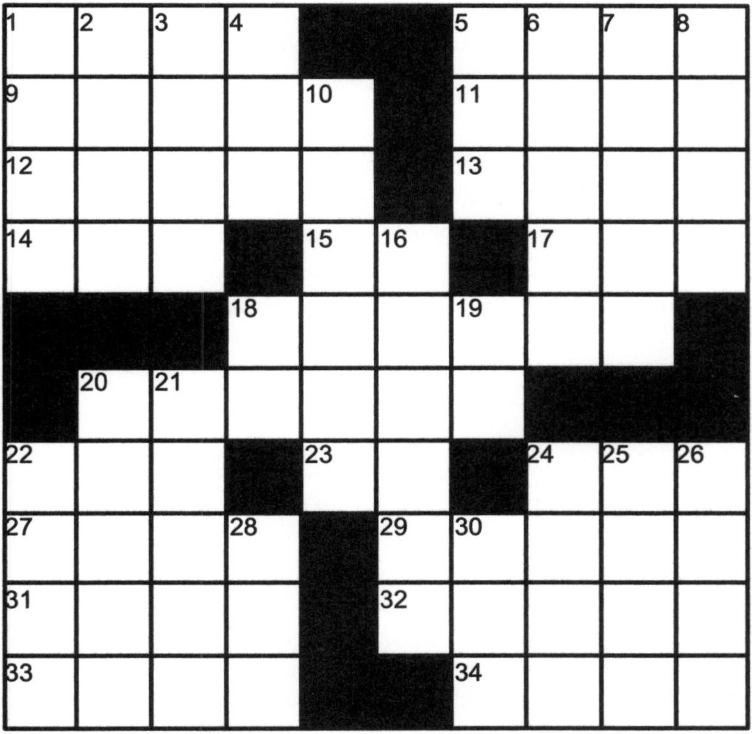

Answers are in the back of the book.

Decode the Quote

*The seven rays on the crown
of the Statue of Liberty represent the seven seas
and continents of the world.*

Fill-in the words that match their definitions. Then complete the solution by placing each letter that corresponds with its matching number into the spaces below. When you're finished, you'll find what President THOMAS JEFFERSON, had to say about Jesus.

Book of maps

___	___	___	___	___
14	1	17	14	10

Hooped petticoat

___	___	___	___
6	7	8	9

___	___	___	___	___
5	17	8	9	3

Musical improvisation

___   ___   ___
12   14   15

Vendetta

___   ___   ___   ___
11   3   13   4

Fanfare

___   ___   ___   ___   ___   ___
2   5   5   16   17   14

1	2	3		4	5	6	1	7	8	9	3	10		5	11			
															,			
12	3	10	13	10		14	7	3		10	8	15	16	17	3			
14	9	4		1	3	9	4		14	17	17		1	5		1	2	3
2	14	16	16	8	9	3	10	10		5	11		15	14	9	.		

Answers are in the back of the book.

Three-Letter Words

"I love you", "I am sorry", "Thank you, God", "You did well", "Let me help"... Three words sincerely spoken can pack a lot of meaning. Each answer in this puzzle is short and sweet – only three letters long!

ACROSS

1 Everyone
4 The Caribbean is one
7 Luau dish
8 Wise bird
9 Tide movement
10 One introduced to society, for short
11 Duet
14 Epoch
17 Pasture sound
18 Cavity
19 Query
20 Cheat

DOWN

1 Jungle critter
2 Toss
3 Ad __
4 Ground
5 Ram's mate
6 Priestly vestment
11 Information to come, for short
12 Used to be
13 Mighty tree
14 Chick holder
15 Sunbeam
16 Tablet download

Kind and Loving

Throughout the Bible, there are many instances of people—people just like us—going out of their way to show kindness and love to others. Match the incident in the first column with the man or woman's name in the second column.

1. God put a mark on him that forbade anyone from murdering him, even though he was a murderer.

a. Philip

2. Priscilla and her husband, Aquila, helped this new believer preach the Gospel with increased knowledge and accuracy.

b. Mary Magdalene

3. This evangelist opened the Scriptures, and baptized, a God-fearing man from Ethiopia.

c. Cain

4. She, wife of Chuza, was among many wealthy women who financially supported Jesus and His disciples.

d. Joanna

5. This aunt of the child-prince Joash hid him and his nurse to protect him from her sister's intent to kill the young prince.

e. Apollos

6. She rejoiced with Mary at the news of her pregnancy, and undoubtedly encouraged the young women during this time.

f. Elizabeth

7. She and another woman arrived early in the morning at Jesus' tomb, intending to anoint His body.

g. Jehosheba

Answers are in the back of the book.

Laughter is Good Medicine

Though we don't think of the Bible as a funny book, there's humor scattered throughout its pages. Match the incident in the first column with the person in the second column.

1. To illustrate how each person possesses unique gifts, this apostle asked his hearers to imagine a body consisting only of an eye or an ear.	a. Jesus
2. A watchman could identify this Old Testament warrior's approach from afar because he drove like a maniac.	b. Sarah
3. He said that before we attempt to correct the faults of others, we correct our own faults, which are like big logs lodged in our eyes.	c. Dagon
4. When the Philistines captured the Ark of God and set it in their temple, they awoke to find that this idol had fallen over in a prostrate position in front of the Ark.	d. Paul
5. Because of her advanced age, the idea that she and her elderly husband could have a child together struck her so funny that she burst out laughing.	e. Balaam
6. To amuse wedding guests, this Old Testament warrior posed a riddle: From an eater, something to eat; out of the strong, something sweet.	f. Jehu
7. God caused this man's donkey to speak to him, as he had allowed money to trump his own good sense.	g. Samson

Answers are in the back of the book.

Big Puzzler

Warning: A few of these are pretty punny!

ACROSS
1 Disconnected
4 Male deer
9 Clammy
12 __ de Janeiro
13 Impressionist painter
14 Hearer
15 Computer keyboard key
16 Stadium
17 Exist
18 Bake shelled eggs
20 Yesterday's dimple
22 Airport abbr.
24 Time period
25 Ambassador's offices
29 Agreed (with)
33 Domestic help
34 Dawdle
36 Salute in Mexico City
37 Undo a knot
39 Tired, with "out"
41 I-dolatry
43 Sodom fleer
44 Sluggish one (archaic)
48 Cries
52 Fuss
53 Son of Cain
55 By way of

56 M.D., for short
57 English tea go-with
58 Sick
59 __ of the Covenant
60 Perceive
61 Allow

DOWN
1 Mined metals
2 You find them in a school
3 Central points
4 Stings
5 Sticky black substance
6 Fresh
7 Style, as in music
8 They're always up to something
9 Flimsy
10 Banjo player Scruggs
11 Maple
19 Prepared
21 Innocence
23 Handy way to communicate
25 Flightless bird
26 Woman's partner
27 Fragment
28 Talk

DOWN CON'T

30 Org. head
31 Adam's wife
32 Male parent
35 It can make your hair stand on end
38 Exodus
40 Common finch
42 Kitchen measurement

44 Pop
45 Smell
46 It's all keyed up
47 Sky light
49 Wicked
50 Heap
51 It's useful in a pinch
54 Brain and spinal cord together (Abbr.)

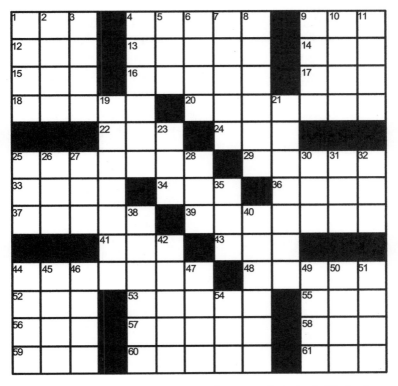

Answers are in the back of the book.

Another Try

If you have a hunch you can do it, give it a go. Sometimes a hunch is God's way of saying, "Now is the time."

It's always a good time to try these things!

ACROSS
2 Friendly
5 Fearless
7 Candid
9 Rely on
11 Aware
13 Dependable
14 Be concerned
16 Please
20 Constant
21 Exultant
22 Respectful
24 Zealous
27 Astute
28 Out-loud grin
31 Gentleness

DOWN
1 Smart
3 Belief in God
4 Nice
6 Thankfulness
8 Enduring
10 Grin
12 Satisfied
14 Level-headed
15 Lighthearted
17 Diplomatic
18 Undertaking
19 Bravery
23 Affection
25 Aid
26 Generosity
29 Look forward to, with "for"
30 Serenity

Answers are in the back of the book.

Decode the Lyrics

There are 972 known musical arrangements of the hymn "Amazing Grace".

Fill-in the words that match their definitions. Then, complete the solution by placing each letter that corresponds with its matching number into the spaces below. When you're finished, you'll complete a stanza from the hymn *"Jesus Loves Even Me"*, by American songwriter, conductor and Gospel singer, PHILIP P. BLISS.

Oh, if there's only one song I can sing
When in His beauty I see the great King...

Donation for the poor

___	___	___	___
5	6	7	4

Progeny

___	___	___	___	___
8	9	13	10	11

Lacking enthusiasm

__	__	__	__	__
19	5	18	14	18

Taurine

__	__	__	__	__	__
16	9	20	3	10	14

Squirm

__	__	__	__	__	__
17	12	3	1	2	14

1	2	3	4		4	2	5	6	6		7	8		4	9	10	11			
																				,
1	2	12	9	13	11	2		14	1	14	12	10	3	1	8		16	14		
"			,																	
	9	2			17	2	5	1		5		17	9	10	18	14	12			
																				!"
1	2	5	1		19	14	4	13	4		6	9	20	14	4		7	14		

Answers are in the back of the book.

Perfectly True

Follow the clues by crossing off words in the grid. Some words might be crossed off by more than one clue. When you are finished, the remaining words form a quotation by RALPH WALDO EMERSON, reading down one column at a time.

1. Cross out names of capital cities.
2. Cross out names of books of the Bible.
3. Cross out articles of clothing.
4. Cross out things you might see in the sky.
5. Cross out names of trees, plants, and flowers.
6. Cross out words denoting size.
7. Cross out words denoting strength.
8. Cross out words that contain two of the letters R, S and T.

MIGHTY	TO	POWERFUL	NOVA
BELT	NUMBERS	CARRY	MOON
THOUGH	FIND	MARK	FIND
PALM	THE	PARIS	POTENT
WE	RIVER	IT	TICKETS
ROME	CLOUDS	MADRID	IT
STARS	BEAUTIFUL	WITH	DRESS
TRAVEL	DAISY	ACTS	OAK
SEAS	WE	ROSE	LILY
THE	HUGE	US	GIGANTIC
WORLD	GREAT	OR	STREAMS
ROBE	WASHINGTON	FERN	NOT
OVER	MUST	WE	GRATITUDE

Saying: _____

Great Stories!

Jesus parables have been defined as earthly stories with heavenly meanings. Match the "earthly story" in the first column with the "heavenly meaning" in the second column.

1. A farmer sows seed in many kinds of soil; some seeds take root, and others do not.

2. A widow pleas for justice; she finally receives it, because the judge realizes she will not give up.

3. A Samaritan who was looked down upon was the only one who stopped to help a man in need.

4. A shepherd discovers that one sheep has wandered away; he leaves to search for it.

5. One man built his house on sand, and it fell; another built on rock, and it withstood the storm.

6. It's an ill-advised builder who starts building before he knows if he's able to complete it!

7. A manager erased his servant's debt, but the servant demanded payment from those owing him.

8. Three servants received money; two invested it and reaped a profit; the third simply returned it.

9. Workers were all paid the same, whether they worked all day or only part of the day.

a. The one we despise may possess more faith, compassion, and generosity than we do.

b. We are to fully use whatever gifts God give us and not let them lie dormant.

c. Firm faith in God will carry us through life's troubles and difficulties.

d. God rewards persistence in prayer; at the right time, He will answer.

e. Discipleship may cost us, and we should know this before we declare ourselves His disciples.

f. Because God forgives us, we must forgive others.

g. God is as generous to new believers as He is to life-long believers.

h. Some who receive God's Word believe; others reject the gift of faith.

i. God will not fail to notice if even one of us strays from faith in Him; and He will look for us.

Answers are in the back of the book.

The Giving Life

There are countless ways to give—this puzzle includes some of them!

ACROSS

1 Uphold
3 Counsel
5 Pardon
6 Improve
11 Divide
14 Togetherness
16 Hear
17 Go ahead of
18 Goodwill
21 Instruct
24 Act compassionately (2 words)
25 Put others __: be magnanimous
26 Pat on __: congratulate (2 words)
27 Go __ for: act on behalf of another (2 words)
28 Cure

DOWN

2 Esteem
4 Contribute with no charge
7 Speak to God on behalf of (2 words)
8 Encourage
9 Construct
10 Direct
12 Respite
13 Compliment
15 Help out (3 words)
19 Thoughtfulness
20 Nourish
22 Soothe
23 Spur on
24 A benediction
26 Spend __ with: visit

Answers are in the back of the book.

Genuine Interest

If you have a hobby you love, give thanks for the blessing that it truly is. Savor the joy it brings to your life, and think of ways your special interest might benefit others, or inspire them to pursue their own passions. In the list below, match the answer with each clue.

ORNITHOLOGIST   BIBLIOPHILE
GEOCACHER   RAPPELLER
GENEALOGIST   APIARIST
PHILATELIST   DELTIOLOGIST
NUMISMATIST   AUDIOPHILE
CRYPTOLOGIST   CALLIGRAPHER

1. Stamp collector: _____

2. Ancestry seeker: _____

3. Code breaker: _____

4. Coin collector: _____

5. Lettering artist: _____

6. Bird observer: _____

7. Beekeeper: _____

8. GPS-armed searcher: _____

9. Cliff descender: _____

10. Book collector: _____

11. Postcard collector: _____

12. Music enthusiast: _____

Answers are in the back of the book.

Two Sides

Put the answer to Clue 1 in box 1. Scramble the letters and drop one letter to answer Clue 2. Write the word in box 2 and the dropped letter in the left-hand box. Scramble the letters and drop one letter to answer Clue 3. Write the word in box 3 and the dropped letter in the right-hand box. Complete each row the same way, starting with a new word. When you're finished, reading vertically on the left, you'll find the name of a disciple who sinned and lost all hope; and on the right, a disciple who sinned, but asked for and received forgiveness.

1. He had a coat of many colors
2. Expects
3. Footwear
4. Uses a blender
5. Shopping __: wild spending
6. Agents, for short
7. Became anxious
8. Most high schoolers

9. Observed
10. Cognizant
11. Pottery, for example
12. Not cooked
13. Declare
14. Glare, transfixed
15. Fill up

	1.	2.	3.	
	4.	5.	6.	
	7.	8.	9.	
	10.	11.	12.	
	13.	14.	15.	

Answers are in the back of the book.

Big Puzzler

With words of six letters or less, you can answer all the clues in this crossword.

ACROSS
1 Rug type
5 Flow's partner
8 Took a chair
11 Upkeep
12 Pod dweller
13 Canal
14 Baker's need
15 Spots
16 Zilch
17 Letter styles
19 Put down
21 Ag. org.
22 King David's composition
24 Obtained
27 Bongo, for one
28 Tending (to)
30 Unkind person
33 Tested
34 City area
35 Baby's bed
36 Mr.'s partner
37 Claw
39 ___ chi
42 Norway's capital
43 Small branches
45 Short form, for short

48 Ship letters
50 Cain's brother
51 Light need
52 Lion name
53 Garden creeper
54 Omaha summer hour
55 Sum up
56 Has lunch

DOWN
1 Tease
2 Chaos
3 Playing field
4 Polite man, for short
5 Climate org.
6 Confusion
7 Elemental
8 Madrid Mrs.
9 Help
10 Beverage
13 Conclusion
18 Dashes
20 Etch in
23 Take to court
24 State official, for short
25 Only
26 Commandment number

DOWN CON'T

27 Genetic code letters
29 Steal
30 Silent
31 Sin
32 Body builder's pride, for short
33 For
35 Shut
38 Birds "thumb"

39 Leg bone
40 Representative
41 Oahu and others
42 Ball
44 Wordless "hi"
45 Pre-K letters
46 Develop
47 Deli order, for short
49 Turf

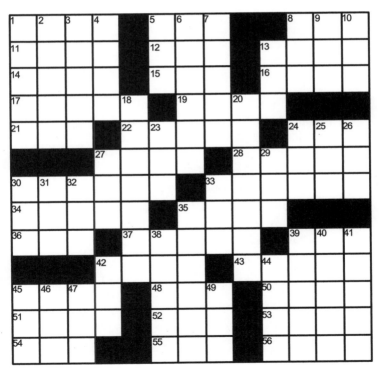

Answers are in the back of the book.

The Battle Won

With God's help, each of these Bible figures bravely confronted their enemies. Choose the right answer for each clue.

1. This Israelite captive in Babylon, along with two others, risked perishing in a fiery furnace rather than bow down to the idol that King Nebuchadnezzar had set up.
   a. Meshach
   b. Daniel
   c. Haman

2. By asking the king for a favor, this Israelite queen put her life on the line for the sake of her people.
   a. Esther b. Sheba c. Deborah

3. This early believer prophesied that the apostle Paul would be arrested if we went to Jerusalem; Paul replied that even if it meant death, he would proceed to Jerusalem and spread the Gospel message.
   a. Priscilla b. Philip c. Agabus

4. King Herod had this early-church leader put to death so he could win the approval of temple leaders who did not accept Jesus Christ.
   a. Peter b. James c. Silas

5. This disciple suffered many trials and was finally exiled to the island of Patmos because of his faithfulness to the Gospel message.
   a. John
   b. Andrew
   c. Philip

6. According to tradition, this disciple was crucified upside down by the Emperor Nero.
   a. James b. Peter c. John

7. His wife chided him for remaining faithful to God, even though he had suffered grievous loss.
   a. Jeremiah b. Ezekiel c. Job

Answers are in the back of the book.

Chance Taken

Many Bible figures took a chance without being certain of the outcome. Match the name in the first column with the chance he or she took in the second column.

1. Jacob

a. He took a chance that, despite God's startling orders to sacrifice his only son, there would be an heir, as God had promised.

2. Noah

b. He took a chance that Jesus would heal his servant, even though he was a gentile.

3. Ruth

c. It must have appeared bizarre to see a man build a boat where there was no water, but this man took a chance and obeyed God's instructions.

4. Abraham

d. When Eli the priest said that God would answer her prayer, she went home content and comforted.

5. Centurion

e. Had his brother changed his mind after all these years, or did he still want to kill him? He took a chance that his brother had changed.

6. Peter

f. Jesus said, "Come," and he stepped out of the boat and onto the water of the Sea of Galilee.

7. Hannah

g. She took a chance by remaining with her mother-in-law; after all, she'd be a foreigner, and perhaps no one would accept her.

Answers are in the back of the book.

Show Me!

Many figures in the Bible said, "Show me!" You'll find a few of them in this puzzle.

ACROSS

1 Competent
5 Land measurement
9 Where Jesus' showed His sacrifice
11 Old Testament idol
12 Bog
13 Caribbean nation
14 Abort
15 Portland locale (Abbr.)
17 "Show me my offense and my __" (Job 13:23 NIV)
18 Made coffee
20 Grass cutting blade
22 Pronoun for Mary or Martha
23 Southern African nation (Abbr.)
24 Caesarea to Nazareth dir.
27 "The __ and the lamb shall feed together" (Isa. 65:25)
29 Loot
31 Sheaf
32 What Jesus showed Thomas, who doubted His resurrection
33 "The Lord is __ to anger" (Nah. 1:3)
34 Jesus __ from the tomb

DOWN

1 Peak
2 Cereal choice
3 "Show me your ways, __, teach me your paths" (Psa. 25:4 NIV)
4 Kind of curve
5 First letters
6 Motive
7 Ill rodent, maybe
8 Dash
10 Summer clothing
16 Bring up again
18 "He shall be like a tree planted __ the rivers" (Psa. 1:3)
19 "Forgive us our debts, as __ forgive our debtors" (Matt. 6:12)
20 Shallow area in a river
21 Large stringed instrument
22 Compass point
24 Taboo (2 words)
25 Offers
26 Otherwise
28 "Harvest truly is plenteous, but the laborers are __" (Matt. 9:37)
30 Golfer's goal

Answers are in the back of the book.

Peace Within

I have learned in whatsoever state I am,
therewith to be content.

Philippians 4:11

Find synonyms for contentment as you unscramble these letters. When you are finished, unscramble the letters in parenthesis for another word of contentment!

1. Y E T E R I N S (__) __ __ __ __ __ __ __

2. C O A T S I N A F I S T

   __ __ __ __ __ __ __ __ (__) __ __ __ __

3. R E U S E L A P __ __ __ __ __ (__) __ __ __ __

4. T O Y J E M E N N __ __ __ __ __ __ __ (__) __ __

5. L I F T U N L F L E M

   __ (__) __ __ __ __ __ __ __ __ __

6. E V E N T H E M I C A

   __ (__) __ __ __ __ __ __ __ __ __ __

7. G I N T H I S __ __ (__) __ __ __ __

   Answer: __ __ __ __ __ __ __

Answers are in the back of the book.

104

Transformations

When you chose to forgive, you are doing yourself a favor. Forgiveness means that you will not let someone else's sin define your life. You will seek strength, healing, and peace.

In the puzzles below, change the first word into the second word of each pair by replacing only one letter at a time. Do not scramble letter order; use only common English words, and no capitalized words.

Example: LOSE, lone, line, fine, FIND

1. HARD
   _____
   _____
   _____
   _____
   SOFT

2. MEAN
   _____
   _____
   _____
   _____
   KIND

3. HATE
   _____
   _____
   _____
   _____
   PITY

4. COLD
   _____
   _____
   _____
   _____
   WARM

5. PAIN
   _____
   _____
   _____
   _____
   HEAL

Answers are in the back of the book.

Who Follows Jesus Word Search

The names below are just a few of Jesus' followers as recorded in the Bible. Find their names hidden forward, backward, horizontally, vertically and diagonally.

ANDREW	PAUL
APOLLOS	PETER
AQUILA	PHILEMON
BARNABAS	PHILIP
BARTHOLOMEW	PHOEBE
CHILDREN	PRISCILLA
CORNELIUS	SAINTS
ETHIOPIAN	SILAS
JAMES	SIMON
JOHN	SINNERS
JUDE	STEPHEN
JULIA	TABITHA
LUKE	THIEF
LYDIA	THOMAS
MARK	TIMOTHY
MARY	TITUS
MATTHEW	YOU
NICODEMUS	ZACCHEUS

```
U A B N E D B G C C G X D R X R F H F A A T
L P X S I E K U L A K X I V L S R E N N I S
U J S O Z C K J H A D Y V Z C X R V L M M H
A T T C F W O T U F Q K H V C M G U O P U A
P H E I I T I D T D H U I O T N H T R N P S
Q O P K A B E C E I E W I A D R H I Q O J U
H M H U A O S T H M T V U L I Y S D L A U I
Z A E T G Z Y C H P U U P B A C J L M X L L
X S N B W H E V R I I S S E I X O O T X I E
D D C I A B G U P W O U O L T S J D W R A N
H C T D E R S N T K Y P L Y Z W H B O C G R
A H X O A C T Z M I K A I W Y E H L R O Q O
R N H F R U P H I L I P Z A Y R C R D N D C
U P M X K Z W L O B P J M A N D J M F H A D
Q R D P P V N K V L N H O I X N V I A F F S
F W N X J O H N V S O D A L X A Q F E I H T
W Z E A I D Y L U Q U M Y T J T F A E G E L
P M J M Y C K E U F Z I E W B M D S A L I S
Y E K N I Z H E L O T F E W X R N O M I S U
I P T V E C L J T E Z H L C W O D P Y S M H
S F P E C R A H U F T M L T N C S T N I A S
S I V A R M D L M T P P B K N O M E L I H P
L M Z F E E S L A I B W R R X Y Y N J N M E
E A R S Z L K M I L U R U A S T E R N V Q O
D S A R Q X J B K H L O C M I B V M A M E C
R T B A R N A B A S C A Y G C X N R Q M C O
```

Answers are in the back of the book.

Bible Foods

Nourishing food was as important, and as necessary, in Bible times as it is today. Use the Bible "grocery list" to complete the puzzle grid; one word has been filled in to get you started.

FOUR LETTERS

CORN   LAMB
EGGS   MILK
FIGS   MINT
FISH   NUTS
         SALT

FIVE LETTERS

BEANS
CUMIN
HONEY
LEEKS
WHEAT

SIX LETTERS

BARLEY   GRAPES
BUTTER   MELONS
CHEESE   OLIVES
GARLIC   ONIONS

SEVEN LETTERS

ALMONDS
LENTILS
MUSTARD
VENISON

Answers are in the back of the book.

Love Is

Each clue suggests a loving action or characteristic. Within the answer word, there is a word that corresponds to the bolded clue-element.
Example:
Large hibernating mammal's self-control:
FOR**BEAR**ANCE

1. Empathy for a **direction-determining device**:

   ___ ___ ___ ___ ___ ___ ___ ___ ___

2. **Serenade** of good fortune: ___ ___ ___ ___ ___ ___ ___ ___ ___

3. Determination not to **disunite**:

   ___ ___ ___ ___ ___ ___ ___ ___ ___ ___ ___ ___

4. Is generous with a **writing instrument**:

   ___ ___ ___ ___ ___ ___ ___ ___ ___

5. A suitable **item for a stage play**:

   ___ ___ ___ ___ ___ ___ ___ ___ ___ ___

6. Friendly **TV channel-provider**:

   ___ ___ ___ ___ ___ ___ ___

7. Not given to boasting in a **canvas shelter**:

   ___ ___ ___ ___ ___ ___ ___ ___ ___ ___ ___ ___ ___

8. **Relating to us**, it's only polite:

   ___ ___ ___ ___ ___ ___ ___ ___ ___

9. Caring **adjacency**:

   ___ ___ ___ ___ ___ ___ ___ ___ ___ ___

10. Helpful **harbor for cruise ships**:

    ___ ___ ___ ___ ___ ___ ___ ___ ___

Answers are in the back of the boo

How They Changed!

God worked big changes in the lives of Bible figures, just as He does in the lives of people today. Match the names in the first column with the change God produced in them in the second column.

1. Abraham

2. Paul

3. Esther

4. Deborah

5. Moses

6. Jeremiah

7. Amos

8. Ruth

9. Mary Magdalene

a. Rural sheepherder and fig farmer turned preacher to the Samaritans, urging morality and righteousness.

b. Hebrew raised in luxury of Pharaoh's household turned sheepherder and later, leader of Israelites.

c. Wealthy, settled landowner in Ur turned nomad as he gathers his household and sets out for Canaan.

d. Pious but immature youth turned outspoken, fiery preacher urging a return to God's laws and worship of Him alone.

e. Moabite girl turned believer in the God of Israel and great-grandmother of King David.

f. Intellectually gifted and classically trained Pharisee turned Christian believer and tireless missionary.

g. Israelite judge who settled disputes between people turned courageous and victorious military leader.

h. Socially scorned sinner turned forgiven, redeemed, and highly esteemed disciple of Jesus.

i. Beautiful and faithful Jewish girl turned wife of King Ahasuerus and queen of Persia.

Answers are in the back of the book.

Good, Better, Best

This puzzle is full of fun things!

ACROSS
1 Doggy door
5 Flyer
9 Volcanic rock
10 Roof panel, perhaps
11 Chariots of Fire, ____ Liddell
12 Strong thread
13 Guidance
15 Wanted poster letters
16 Liberty
18 Conversations with God
21 Med. test
22 Sports team
26 In a tilted position
28 Good expectation
29 Little Miss Muffet's meal
30 Paradise
31 Historical time periods
32 Lease

DOWN
1 Pest
2 Shortening
3 Tel __
4 Soothe
5 Arrow launcher
6 Homeric saga
7 "Adventures of Tintin" ape
8 Imagine
10 Is at the helm
14 Old staircase sounds
17 Old Testament queen
18 Amity
19 Happen again
20 Ancient Greek market-place
23 Traveled by car
24 What you do with a gift
25 Delivered by post
27 Jewel case contents, for short

Rhyme Time

Your sanctuary provides you a space apart from the daily routine, the demands of others, and the chaos of the world around you. It is in its presence that you gain strength, quietness, and peace of mind to carry with you wherever you go.

Each clue can below be answered with two rhyming words.

Example:
Optimist's question to moaner: **W H Y   S I G H?**

1. Sanctuary for Poe's bird:

   __ __ __ __ __   __ __ __ __ __

2. Rent tranquility: __ __ __ __ __   __ __ __ __ __ __

3. Blessing spot: __ __ __ __ __ __   __ __ __ __ __

4. More elevated longing:

   __ __ __ __ __ __   __ __ __ __ __ __

5. Discovered garden spot:

   __ __ __ __ __   __ __ __ __ __ __

6. Grab time away: __ __ __ __   __ __ __ __ __

7. A search for respite:__ __ __ __   __ __ __ __ __ __

8. Reduced tension:__ __ __ __   __ __ __ __ __ __ __

9. Attract amazement:__ __ __ __   __ __ __

10. Sense authenticity: __ __ __ __   __ __ __ __

Answers are in the back of the book.

114

Who Said It?

For each Bible quote, pick the right speaker and circumstance from the choices given.

1. "I know that my redeemer liveth."
   a. Jonah in the belly of a fish
   b. Job in the midst of misery
   c. Mary Magdalene at the open tomb

2. "Blessed are the peacemakers: for they shall be called the children of God."
   a. Jesus in the Sermon on the Mount
   b. King David as he declared victory over his foes.
   c. The apostle Paul as he urged believers to settle disputes.

3. "Come and see."
   a. Caleb when he reported back to Moses about the Promised Land.
   b. Philip when Nathanael sneered at anything good coming out of Nazareth.
   c. Eve to Adam when she saw how pleasant the forbidden fruit appeared.

4. "Lord, I have heard by many of this man, how much evil he hath done to thy saints at Jerusalem."
   a. Hezekiah after reading Sennacherib's taunting letter.
   b. Joseph praying about King Herod's murderous threats.
   c. Ananias upon being asked to visit Saul of Tarsus.

5. "Against thee, thee only, have I sinned, and done this evil in thy sight."
   a. King David confessing his sins of adultery and murder.
   b. A Roman soldier at the foot of the cross.
   c. Apostle Paul after his conversion, repenting his persecution of Christians.

6. "Lord, now lettest thou thy servant depart in peace, according to thy word."
   a. Moses' confession of faith as he breathed his last.
   b. Simeon's proclamation when he saw the infant Jesus.
   c. The frail apostle John's prayer of acceptance when he was in exile on Patmos.

7. "I advise you: Leave these men alone! ... For if their purpose or activity is of human origin, it will fail. But if it is from God, you will not be able to stop these men."
   a. The Pharisee Gamaliel addressing the Sanhedrin council concerning the apostles' teaching.
   b. Roman captain of the guard trying to calm the crowd demanding the arrest of Paul and Silas.
   c. Believer Aquila's defense of the disciples who had come to spread the gospel message in Corinth.

Answers are in the back of the book.

Time With GOD Word Search

*More than half of Americans say
they pray at least once a day.*

Each of the words below lists just one of the ways
that we can spend time with God. Search for the
words forward, backward, horizontally, vertically
and diagonally.

ACCEPT	PRAY
ACT	PREACH
ASK	QUIET TIME
BELIEVE	READ THE BIBLE
FIND	REPENT
FORGIVE	REST
GIVE	SACRIFICE
GIVE THANKS	SEEK
GLORIFY	SERVE
GROW	SHARE
HOPE	SING
KNEEL	SURRENDER
LEARN	TEACH
LISTEN	TITHE
LOVE	TRUST
MEMORIZE	WALK
OBEY	WORK
PRAISE	WORSHIP

```
S  A  C  R  I  F  I  C  E  M  G  T  P  E  W  A  L  K  P  E
T  R  U  S  T  X  W  N  X  Y  I  Q  D  G  A  S  K  K  N  W
Q  T  S  E  R  A  O  O  E  T  E  R  Z  W  C  Z  L  Q  A  N
U  R  E  K  L  S  R  R  H  V  Z  F  I  Y  C  S  W  W  A  O
I  T  T  U  J  W  S  E  I  S  I  Z  F  V  E  T  F  P  K  R
K  H  F  E  Z  U  H  G  O  R  H  I  I  R  P  Q  P  R  E  O
N  K  U  T  A  A  I  O  I  F  L  A  V  N  T  O  H  A  B  B
E  R  P  C  Y  C  P  D  T  Y  L  E  R  H  Q  R  D  Y  T  E
E  O  N  A  Q  J  H  X  O  L  T  D  C  E  W  T  D  R  P  Y
L  W  R  H  Y  H  G  W  J  Z  G  A  H  J  H  U  N  E  U  Q
E  H  A  H  S  J  B  V  P  Z  E  D  Y  E  K  L  I  X  U  S
K  F  E  Z  I  M  A  H  K  R  D  E  B  J  R  I  F  I  Z  K
T  V  L  D  N  X  X  S  P  X  W  I  E  E  U  S  E  E  H  N
X  U  T  S  G  G  H  G  K  E  B  S  D  E  L  T  Y  Z  N  A
L  O  V  E  T  C  T  G  V  L  I  N  V  M  T  E  F  I  F  H
P  S  E  E  K  N  Z  I  E  A  E  E  D  I  Z  N  I  R  Z  T
K  V  P  H  E  A  G  H  R  R  I  Y  M  W  X  D  R  O  R  E
V  Y  O  P  N  R  J  P  R  L  P  E  V  X  O  O  O  M  D  V
S  N  E  H  O  P  E  U  E  F  J  Y  Z  B  P  R  L  E  F  I
G  R  L  F  Q  G  S  B  N  K  S  D  F  V  K  H  G  M  W  G
```

Answers are in the back of the book.

Decode the Quote

At the age of 14, Ralph Waldo Emerson was the youngest student in his class at Harvard.

Fill-in the words that match their definitions. Then, complete the solution by placing each letter that corresponds with its matching number into the spaces below. When you're finished, you'll find what RALPH WALDO EMERSON had to say about freedom.

A king's ransom

___ ___ ___ ___ ___ ___ ___
 1   2   3   7   13 16 11

Forlorn

___ ___ ___ ___
 14 10 13 18

Shimmy

___ ___ ___ ___ ___ ___
 4   9   14 14 10 11

Middle Eastern sesame candy

$\_$	$\_$	$\_$	$\_$	$\_$	$\_$
5	6	10	8	6	5

Memorial bugle call

$\_$	$\_$	$\_$	$\_$
7	6	12	15

Noah's challenge

$\_$	$\_$	$\_$	$\_$	$\_$
1	10	2	2	17

1	2	3		4	5	6	7		6	8	6	9	10		7	5	11
													,				
12	10	2	13	14	5		2	3		15	6	9	10			2	3
									,								
10	6	16	17		2	3		10	9	1	11			9	1		
										?							
1	3	11	11	17	2	18		1	6	9	10						

Answers are in the back of the book.

119

Books Of The Bible Match Up

Which verse belongs in which book? Match each verse to the book of the Bible it comes from by drawing a line connecting the two.

1. For God so loved the world, that he gave his only begotten Son, that whosoever believeth in him should not perish, but have everlasting life.

a. MICAH

2. I will praise thee; for I am fearfully and wonderfully made: marvellous are thy works; and that my soul knoweth right well.

b. 1 CORINTHIANS

3. God is love; and he that dwelleth in love dwelleth in God, and God in him.

c. 2 CORINTHIANS

4. The Lord thy God in the midst of thee is mighty; he will save, he will rejoice over thee with joy; he will rest in his love, he will joy over thee with singing.

d. JOHN

5. Whether therefore ye eat, or drink, or whatsoever ye do, do all to the glory of God.

e. 1 JOHN

6. What doth the Lord require of thee, but to do justly, and to love mercy, and to walk humbly with thy God?

f. ZEPHANIAH

7. Therefore if any man be in Christ, he is a new creature: old things are passed away; behold, all things are become new.

g. PSALM

Answers are in the back of the book.

It All Adds Up!

Find the word each of the three clues have in common. Write it in the blank to the right. These three solutions form a fourth vertical puzzle. The numbers indicate the number of letters in each solution word. The + tells you the word's position.

For example: + **mate**, + **food** and **lost** + is **SOUL**.

+ brain   (4)   + _____
+ dog
black +

power +   (4)   + _____
worth +
gut +

heart +   (4)   + _____
home +
sea +

Final Answer: (4)   _____

Hint: God is love. 1 John 4:8

BOOKS OF THE BIBLE
Word Search

"Goodbye" came from "Godby" which came from
"God be with you."

Each of the book names in the list below are found
in the Bible. Search for them forward, backward,
horizontally, vertically and diagonally.

ACTS
COLOSSIANS
DANIEL
DEUTERONOMY
EPHESIANS
EXODUS
EZEKIEL
FIRST PETER
GALATIANS
GENESIS
HOSEA
ISAIAH
JOEL
JOHN
JONAH
JOSHUA

JUDGES
LAMENTATIONS
LEVITICUS
LUKE
MALACHI
MARK
MATTHEW
NUMBERS
PHILEMON
PHILIPPIANS
PROVERBS
PSALMS
REVELATIONS
ROMANS
TITUS

```
I  S  A  I  A  H  W  Q  P  M  P  H  D  G  U  H  G  U  A  M
L  E  V  I  T  I  C  U  S  H  G  H  A  C  I  G  A  M  I  L
A  G  E  N  E  S  I  S  A  K  I  X  N  L  Y  Z  L  A  R  A
F  J  O  H  N  S  U  J  C  X  W  L  I  K  Q  U  A  T  N  M
B  I  R  O  M  A  N  S  T  J  B  Z  E  L  C  G  T  T  C  E
K  T  R  E  K  Q  A  Z  S  G  O  D  L  M  F  L  I  H  X  N
A  J  O  S  V  J  M  D  H  B  O  S  X  N  O  P  A  E  Y  T
X  E  L  D  T  E  O  A  U  M  F  O  H  M  B  N  N  W  M  A
B  X  V  U  F  P  L  N  L  S  O  S  F  U  A  A  S  N  P  T
T  O  Y  T  H  O  E  A  A  A  E  Y  J  F  A  R  B  U  H  I
M  D  Z  L  H  T  H  T  T  H  C  C  X  F  L  M  K  M  I  O
L  U  S  M  H  R  V  X  E  I  L  H  A  A  D  Q  U  B  L  N
P  S  E  Z  E  K  I  E  L  R  O  A  I  P  H  B  C  E  I  S
S  N  Q  P  R  O  V  E  R  B  S  N  Z  Y  J  E  F  R  P  Y
A  J  U  D  G  E  S  S  T  X  X  B  S  B  X  O  K  S  P  H
L  H  H  G  J  B  T  I  T  U  S  V  I  L  U  K  E  N  I  O
M  T  M  A  Y  W  F  E  I  Q  C  V  W  V  Y  G  Z  L  A  S
S  D  E  U  T  E  R  O  N  O  M  Y  G  X  W  K  Y  P  N  E
Z  B  Z  U  I  U  D  B  P  C  O  L  O  S  S  I  A  N  S  A
V  E  J  X  N  P  F  E  P  H  E  S  I  A  N  S  Y  O  U  K
```

Answers are in the back of the book.

Make-A-Word

Yes, Jesus Loves Me!

As a young boy lay dying, his Sunday School teacher comforted him with the words of a simple poem, "Jesus loves me! This I know…" This scene takes place in the book, *Say and Seal*. In 1860, it was the bestselling fiction book in the country. The book was written by Susan Arthur, but the poem was penned by her sister, Anna B. Warner. In 1871, the words were put to music by William B. Bradbury.

JESUS LOVES ME! THIS I KNOW…

How many new words can you make from the letters of the six words that begin this popular hymn? If you find more than 150 give yourself a pat on the back!

_____
_____
_____
_____
_____
_____
_____
_____
_____
_____
_____
_____
_____
_____

Possibilities are in the back of the book.

Presidential Quotation Jumble

Arrange the letters in each column into the boxes directly above them to form words. When you've aligned them correctly, you will discover what CALVIN COOLIDGE had to say about worship.

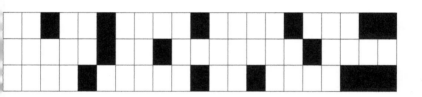

T	T	G	I	N	B	E	N	I	W	O	T	S	H	N	P	M	W	H	A	T
B	H	E	Y	S		O	O	L	Y		R	H	E	G	R	O	E	N		
I	E		I		T	G		N		W	O		I			T				

A Pilgrim's Journey
Trivia Quiz

Offer unto God thanksgiving.
Psalm 50:14

How much do you really know about the Pilgrims who landed in the New World on November 11, 1620? Test your knowledge with the trivia below!

1. Where did the Mayflower first land in the New World?
   a) Plymouth Rock   b) Cape Cod   c) Disney World

2. Which ship was supposed to sail with the Mayflower, but broke down shortly after setting sail?
   a) Puritan's Pride   b) Speedwell   c)Galwaithe

3. What port did the Pilgrims depart from?
   a) Dartmouth, England   b) Plymouth, England
   c) Amsterdam, Netherlands

4. What animals traveled with the 102 passengers on the Mayflower?
   a) 2 dogs   b) 3 horses
   c) a dozen chickens and 2 roosters   d) a, b and c

5. The Pilgrims were also known as_____.
   a) Puritans   b) Separatists   c) Quakers   d) all three

6. Upon arrival in the New World, the Pilgrims signed a governing document known as the Mayflower _____.
   a) Contract   b) Covenant   c) Compact

7. Which person is a descendant of those on the Mayflower?
   a) Franklin D. Roosevelt   b) Marilyn Monroe
   c) Orson Wells   d) all three

8. Which food was served at the first Thanksgiving?
   a) turkey   b) potatoes   c) codfish   d) all three

9. From which tribe were the native Americans who shared the first Thanksgiving with the settlers?
   a) Squanto   b) Seneca   c) Wampanoag

10. Thanksgiving trivia: Before being harvested, a ripe cranberry can bounce this high.
    a) one inch   b) four inches   c) twelve inches

Answers are in the back of the book.

Decode the Lyrics

Fill-in the words that match their definitions. Then complete the solution by placing each letter that corresponds with its matching number into the spaces in the grid below. When you are finished, you'll find KATHERINE LEE BATES request for God's blessings in the lyrics of "America, The Beautiful".

OPPOSITE OF ELDERLY

___	___	___	___	___
7	9	17	15	8

TALENT

___	___	___	___	___
14	13	1	5	4

HOT WATER

___	___	___	___	___
16	11	3	1	2

HOME

—	—	—	—	—
1	18	9	10	3

HOLIDAY SPICE

—	—	—	—	—
6	13	9	19	3

DOMAIN

—	—	—	—	—	—	—
12	1	18	5	11	1	11

							!								!				
1	2	3	4	5	6	1			1	2	3	4	5	6	1				
2	1	7		8	9	10		11	12	7		8	9	13	10				
					,														
4	3	14	5	15	3		11	5	13	13		1	13	13					
																			,
16	17	6	6	3	16	16		18	3		15	9	18	13	3	15	3	16	16
1	15	10		3	19	3	4	7		8	1	5	15		10	5	19	5	15	3

Answers are in the back of the book.

America The Beautiful Word Search

Each of the words in the list below are found in the lyrics of "America, the Beautiful." Search for them forward, backward, horizontally, vertically and diagonally.

ALABASTER	HUMAN
AMBER	LIFE
AMERICA	LOVED
BEAUTIFUL	MERCY
BROTHERHOOD	PATRIOT
CITIES	PILGRIM
COUNTRY	PLAIN
CROWN	SEA
DREAM	SHED
FEET	SHINING
FRUITED	SKIES
GLEAM	SOUL
GOD	SPACIOUS
GOOD	TEARS
GRACE	THY
GRAIN	WAVES
HEROES	WILDERNESS

```
Y  G  B  M  S  G  O  D  C  R  R  E  T  S  A  B  A  L  A  B
G  B  M  E  R  C  Y  Z  X  L  W  A  V  E  S  C  I  O  M  W
P  D  E  M  D  O  O  G  V  H  A  X  C  Y  R  T  N  U  O  C
A  O  A  A  Y  L  S  H  F  L  O  M  R  S  C  W  M  T  U  X
T  T  E  V  U  Z  H  P  X  J  L  X  B  C  S  O  U  L  A  C
R  P  B  S  V  T  L  A  A  U  R  D  Y  E  J  N  W  O  R  C
I  A  A  Y  Q  N  I  U  R  C  L  L  F  T  R  U  Y  P  Q  Y
O  G  H  J  I  R  G  F  F  L  I  U  O  A  C  I  R  E  M  A
T  T  N  A  Z  Q  F  T  U  U  A  O  K  H  S  E  I  T  I  C
D  D  L  I  V  U  L  C  M  L  E  C  U  P  H  U  M  A  N  G
R  P  O  E  N  S  T  O  I  I  S  K  T  S  J  E  S  D  R  X
E  T  R  O  D  I  S  H  V  O  R  Z  O  C  E  U  K  A  U  T
A  R  J  E  H  V  H  E  E  E  B  G  T  C  B  Q  I  F  C  P
M  L  H  T  V  R  V  S  N  I  D  D  L  K  Z  N  E  C  J  E
V  S  S  X  J  P  E  E  R  R  H  M  E  I  N  O  S  Q  S  A
N  S  H  E  G  B  T  H  F  U  E  Y  S  T  P  M  P  P  I  E
E  R  M  J  O  T  K  N  T  K  H  D  C  C  I  M  A  P  N  C
F  A  Y  R  K  R  E  N  N  O  N  L  L  W  J  U  L  E  E  A
I  E  B  J  Z  C  E  E  N  I  R  C  F  I  L  Q  R  W  L  R
L  T  S  M  T  R  T  H  F  I  K  B  R  S  W  U  T  F  O  G
```

Answers are in the back of the book.

Bible Trivia Quiz

Circle the correct answer. (Hint: there may be more than one!)

1. The number of books in the modern Old Testament is 39. But in the Hebrew Bible, there were only 24. The Minor Prophets were grouped together as one book entitled:
   a) Lesser Prophets b) The Twelve c) Other Prophets

2. "Testament" (as in Old Testament and New Testament) means:
   a) Message   b) Covenant   c) Contract

3. What book do most scholars believe to be the oldest book of the Bible?
   a) Psalms   b) Genesis   c) Job

4. What language was the Bible originally written in?
   a) Hebrew   b) Aramaic   c) Greek

5. The Bible was written over a span of how many years
   a) 1500   b) 2000   c) 500

6. Which book of the Bible never mentions the word "God"?
   a) Psalm   b) Malachi   c) Esther

7. Over 40 different authors wrote the Bible. Which one wrote the most books?
   a) Moses   b) Paul   c) Jesus

Answers are in the back of the book.

It All Adds Up!

*The words "under God" were added to the
Pledge of Allegiance in June of 1954.*

Find the word each of the three clues have in common.
Write it in the blank to the right. These three solutions
form a fourth vertical puzzle. The numbers indicate the
number of letters in each solution word. The + tells you
the word's position.
For example: + **mate**, + **food** and **lost** + is **SOUL**.

+ arm   (4)   + _____
+ stick
stock +

wireless +   (5)   + _____
+ trap
Mickey +

+ side   (4)   + _____
down +
+ billy

Final Answer: (6)   _____

Hint: Ephesians 3:21

Answers are in the back of the book.

What's In A Name?

The shortest name in the Bible is Og
(King of Bashan) in Numbers 21:33.

The longest name in the Bible is: Mahershalalhashbaz. Born to Isaiah and "the prophetess," this son is mentioned in Isaiah 8:1,3-4. His name means "He has made haste to the plunder!"

How many words can you make from Isaiah's son's name?

MAHERSHALALHASHBAZ

_____
_____
_____
_____
_____
_____
_____
_____
_____
_____
_____
_____
_____
_____
_____

Possibilities are in the back of the book.

Presidential Quotation Jumble

Arrange the letters in each column into the boxes directly above them to form words. When you've aligned them correctly, you will discover what President ABRAHAM LINCOLN had to say about faith.

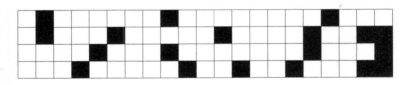

A	N	Y	A	N	T	H	R	U	C	E	A	V	E	O	V	G	A	D	O	W
S	A	C	O	N	H	E	T	E	H	D	S	L	E	O	K	E	U	N	D	
I		T	A	T	N	C	E		L	O	N	C	N	I	S		O	P		
I		M			O	O			I			O	N				H			

Answers are in the back of the book.

Decode the Quote

Fill-in the words that match their definitions. Then, complete the solution by placing each letter that corresponds with its matching number into the spaces below. When you're finished, you'll discover what president GEORGE WASHINGTON had to say about what you should do with your life.

Possible Leviathan

___	___	___	___	___
14	15	2	17	4

Hide

___	___	___	___
1	2	5	3

Swiss song

___	___	___	___	___
8	9	10	4	17

Diatribe

15	2	7	2	12	13	6	4

Handle

15	11	17	16

1	2	3	4		5	6	7	4		8	9	6		2	7	4
10	9	11	12	13		14	15	2	16		13	9	10			
														—		
14	2	12	16	5		8	9	6		16	9		10	9		
16	15	4	12		10	9		11	16		14	11	16	15		
2	17	17		8	9	6	7		5	16	7	4	12	13	16	15

Answers are in the back of the book.

Animals Of The Bible Word Search

In the state of Louisiana there are nearly 2 million alligators. That is about 1 for every 3 people that live in the state.

Each one of the animals listed below is mentioned in the Bible. Track them down forward, backward, horizontally, vertically and diagonally.

BAT
BEETLE
BEHEMOTH
CAMEL
CHAMELEON
DEER
DOVE
EAGLE
FERRET
FISH
FLEA
FOX
FROG
GNAT
GOAT
GRASSHOPPER
HART
HORSE
LAMB

LEOPARD
LEVIATHAN
LION
LIZARD
LOCUST
OSSIFRAGE
PARTRIDGE
PYGARG
RAM
SCORPION
SPARROW
SPIDER
STORK
TORTOISE
TURTLEDOVE
UNICORN
WHALE
WORM

```
V  M  H  E  Z  D  E  E  R  Y  Z  W  H  A  L  E  Z  Q  R  S
Z  C  A  T  P  A  R  T  R  I  D  G  E  L  A  M  B  U  T  R
C  V  R  T  M  T  D  E  D  X  T  A  B  W  A  U  A  O  G  P
K  K  T  Q  E  U  K  N  J  D  L  B  M  G  H  E  R  R  Y  S
O  I  U  A  C  R  U  N  I  C  O  R  N  R  B  K  L  G  O  E
W  E  S  I  O  T  R  O  T  A  E  I  O  A  P  F  A  F  M  H
T  I  E  S  V  L  Q  E  L  G  A  E  D  S  G  R  S  Q  U  G
P  C  H  A  M  E  L  E  O  N  W  C  K  S  G  A  O  V  I  F
F  V  Q  L  M  D  Y  W  B  T  F  D  R  H  N  O  I  L  E  P
S  G  O  R  F  O  O  S  F  B  A  I  H  O  E  M  N  R  N  Y
X  P  L  W  G  V  A  B  O  T  E  N  B  P  G  N  R  A  N  C
A  E  A  O  C  E  S  Z  Z  L  I  C  G  P  D  E  H  E  A  S
Y  R  B  R  J  Y  N  X  T  V  R  A  T  E  T  T  G  M  C  Z
L  I  Z  A  R  D  H  E  A  W  D  M  C  R  A  A  O  O  H  C
R  F  F  O  K  O  E  W  O  R  T  E  J  I  R  I  R  D  Y  I
E  N  E  I  G  B  W  R  A  S  W  L  V  F  S  P  M  B  I  P
D  H  S  J  S  H  M  P  U  K  T  E  I  F  I  D  E  M  U  N
I  M  R  A  Q  H  O  C  U  A  L  S  X  O  J  D  R  V  A  B
P  G  O  J  K  E  O  K  O  W  S  O  N  U  M  M  W  R  O  R
S  M  H  N  L  L  E  G  I  O  F  B  E  H  E  M  O  T  H  D
```

Answers are in the back of the book.

American Hymnists

The oldest Christian hymn whose author is known.
It was written in the year 200.
Shepherd of Tender Youth, written by Clement of Alexandria.

Solve this puzzle's clues by completing the name of a famous American hymn writer or the title of one of their timeless worship songs.

ACROSS

1) Fanny _____
4) "_____ Like Jesus"
7) "To God Be The _____"
8) "Pass Me Not, O _____ Savior"
9) "Nothing But The _____"
10) "Sunshine In My _____"
11) _____ Bliss
13) "_____ In The Arms of Jesus"
15) _____ J. Kirkpatrick
17) "_____ Up, _____ Up For Jesus"
18) "Away In A _____"
19) "Jesus Loves _____ Me"
20) "Lord, I'm Coming _____"
24) Eliza _____
25) "In The _____"
27) _____ Henry Hopkins, Jr.
28) "I Am Not Skilled To_____"
29) "Lead Me To _____"
30) "_____ Persuaded"

DOWN

2) "_____ Assurance"
3) "Going Up _____"
5) "My _____ Has Found A Resting Place"
6) "_____ Him, Praise Him"
8) "The _____ Train"
12) Robert _____
13) "His Eye Is On The _____"
14) "Blessed Be The ____"
16) "Behold The ____ Of Galilee"
17) "'Tis So _____ To Trust In Jesus"
20) "When We All Get To _____"
21) Charles Austin _____
22) "Shall We _____ At The River"
23) "_____ Paid It All"
26) "We Three _____"

Influential American Christians Match-Up

The name "Quakers" originates from the fact that early worshippers would "quake with the spirit of God."

Write the number of each description in front of the name of the woman of God who matches it.

1) First female American missionary to work overseas, she strived to educate girls in India and Burma.

2) Born a slave named Isabella Baumfree, this woman become a famous itinerant preacher.

3) Quaker lay speaker and author of the bestseller, *The Christian's Secret to a Happy Life*.

4) Member of the first class to accept female medical students at Cornell University, her one-bed clinic in India grew into one of the largest hospitals in the world.

5) In the late 1700s, she was the first American woman to earn a living as a writer. Her most famous work is *View of Religious Opinions*.

6) Born a slave, she supported her family by as a cook and washer woman and later became the first female African American evangelist.

7) Her song, "Blessed Assurance", was sung in two Academy Award winning movies.

8) Only 4'3", this diminutive woman was a well-known missionary to China for almost 40 years.

    a. ___ Lottie Moon

    b. ___ Hannah Adams

    c. ___ Hannah Whithall Smith

    d. ___ Amanda Berry Smith

    e. ___ Fanny Crosby

    f. ___ Sojourner Truth

    g. ___ Ida Scudder

    h. ___ Annie Hasseltine Judson

Answers are in the back of the book.

Presidential Quotation Jumble

Arrange the letters in each column into the boxes directly above them to form words. When you've aligned them correctly, you will discover what ANDREW JACKSON had to say about the Bible.

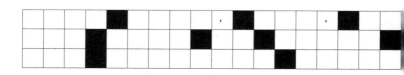

T	H	R	T	R	E	C	U	K	L	I	S	I	H	I	S	H	S
T	U	E		R	B	O	O	B	O	N	C	W	R	E	C	I	S
O	H	A			O	P	K					R			T		

Answers are in the back of the book.

It All Adds Up!

Find the word each of the three clues have in common.
Write it in the blank to the right. These three solutions
form a fourth vertical puzzle. The numbers indicate the
number of letters in each solution word. The + tells you
the word's position.

For example: + **mate**, + **food** and **lost** + is **SOUL**.

+ smith   (4)   + _____
pass +
after +

+ way   (4)   + _____
sleep +
jay +

camel +   (4)   + _____
+ line
+ do

Final Answer: (5)   _____

              Hint: Our Hope

God Is Love Word Search

Find the reading's **bolded words** in the word search puzzle.

Many of us grew up **hearing stories** and **watching movies** about valiant princes and **beautiful** princesses. They all lived **happily** ever after! We longed for the day when that **special** someone would come into **our lives** and love us **faithfully** and **exclusively** forever. That's **what** we knew about love!

As we **mature**, however, we **realize** that there are many **kinds of** love. **Romantic** love, **of course**...but also love **between** parent and child...love for **our friends**...love among those **belonging** to the same **congregation**...love of **country**...love of **life itself**. The word "love" is **packed** with meaning, **emotion**, and **positive images**.

Yet more meanings **unfold** with the **passing years**. Your love **grows** and **deepens**. Each day, **express** your love by showing love to the **people** with whom you **share** your life, and **thank them** for all the ways they show their love to you. Love is a **gift**, an **adventure**. Never shut **yourself** away from the **blessing** of loving and being loved, because "**God is love**" (1 John 4:8).

```
Y E N O U R F R I E N D S I E I H F D X F A
C M X U D N V B L E S S I N G K U D O F D H
A O A E X C L U S I V E L Y U V L T W V E U
Q T T F Y Q Y J X C E O T J R O P V E A D G
C I B C B E T W E E N C F V F K Q N R W M H
G O G O D I S L O V E L C N O V T I Q R A K
P N R E V P X U V G E B U U X U N H L P S F
G M F V G L O G L S G I F T R G S D P F V O
P R P N X E E N T R F J R E S R G I Y I U P
W R O L O N G I F G P L C T A I L I Y R A C
U S L W T T E Q F I O F O E F Y M U L C F I
H C H T S F D B E N P R Y W I Z X I K V F T
U J S A I Q L X G G I G L A U S V E G C V N
Y D P L R V H E R E N E C U E E D D L O A A
J A E G T E D Q S I S M Z G S B B E U N A M
S M C O B I W U S R K L A P M O E E F G H O
Y B I F K T G S U S K M B K O R L P I R Y R
L K A G A G A O O C I P T I J O O E T E O C
L C L S D P C V A E K E T N F J N N U G U U
U S D E Y F V M V E Y O W D I E G S A A R E
F S H M O T Q I Z R O P U S A O I B E T S R
H E Y L H G T I T Q T L O O L N N M B I E U
T R P V L I L N R A P E Q F Z R G V X O L T
I P H O S A U K H Y R I N H G O W R A N F A
A X D O E O H W A T C H I N G M O V I E S M
F E P R C X Z D T H A N K T H E M G U B O J
```

Answers are in the back of the book.

God's Promise

As described in Exodus 32:15, the Ten Commandments were inscribed on both sides, front and back.

Find the answer to each crossword clue by looking up the Bible verse. In the grid, write the corresponding gift God promises you.

ACROSS
3. Acts 3:20
6. Psalm 16:11
8. Psalm 39:7
10. Rom. 5:8
11. Psalm 23:6
14. Heb. 6:19
16. Acts 2:17
17. Psalm 147:3
19. Psalm 119:105
20. Rom. 5:2
22. John 3:16
23. Eph. 4:32
26. Deut. 31:6
27. Ex. 15:2
28. Psalm 48:14

DOWN
1. James 1:5
2. Isaiah 40:29
4. Psalm 71:21
5. Prov. 10:22
7. Prov. 19:21
9. Phil. 4:7
12. Psalm 40:3
13. 1 Cor. 15:57
14. Psalm 91:11
15. 2 Pet. 3:13
18. James 1:3
21. Psalm 33:8
23. Rom. 10:17
24. 1 Pet. 5:7
25. Ez. 36:26 (2 words)

Answers are in the back of the book.

Women Of The Bible Word Search

Each one of these women is mentioned in the Bible.
Find them in the word puzzle, written forward, backward,
horizontally, vertically and diagonally.

ANNA	MARTHA
ASENATH	MARY
BASEMATH	MICHAL
BATHSHEBA	MIRIAM
DEBORAH	NAAMAH
DELILAH	NAOMI
DORCAS	PRISCILLA
ELIZABETH	RACHEL
ESTHER	RAHAB
EVE	REBECCA
HAGAR	RIZPAH
HANNAH	RUTH
JEZEBEL	SARAH
JOANNA	TABITHA
JUDITH	TAMAR
LEAH	TAPHATH

```
T R N A O M I Z D M L A H C I M W U Y G J C
O E I F J O M O Y N R Y E M A L R E H T S E
Q C O Z Z Q Y L B H N L L H T A M E S A B
Q F I P P H W G G Y T T C Z I D R O R L Y A
C Z R H G A V Y X S H O A N P Z V J A T K J
P D J A J X H K L N W B S M V P A X A M T P
I Y U L C O S L R C B A D A A Z G B A T H Y
Q U V I Z H A G B G U H H L C R L R E R O I
T X D L R H E N D G H A K R T R Y Q J T A C
Z X D E B F S L N N R R Y K A E O Q F B H E
H B C D M O P Y Z A A I R B M G N D A L Q B
A L Y Z X F X D R L G V E K A S A N Q K S M
R C E N R R B N L B A A B X P G T H N Q I I
O G Z A N B E X C S F X E B E A U W V R S B
B F W A H S P I J P M M C V E H F B I T T T
E E T S X A H A M A A N C D M T Y A M A A Y
D O D R Y R A B Q R U J A U U R M W Z P S A
K Q E T O A Q K G E E E A A W A P E H J Q H
B A K Y P H X Q X H J X L B N M B A H G F T
T D Z P Q G H V H U A L Y N E L T F G A N I
G W E Z T T D A D X I N A X S H E E Y W G B
Y V G T A R Q I N C F H N B I J S B P B Z A
E W F N U M T B S C C C T A P J A H E T J T
X M E T S H T I F D B P M Z H X H J T Z Q N
N S H G W S R B Z O M M X O V K V Z S A E D
A J R K P P U A Z D V S Y G R S V X W E B J
```

Answers are in the back of the book.

Which Book?

Each of the clues describes something from one specific book of the Bible. Complete the puzzle by writing that biblical book's name in the grid.

ACROSS

1. 4 Horsemen of the Apocalypse (abbr.)
3. Jesus meets the woman at the well
6. Not-so-great friends: Bildad, Zophar, Eliphaz
7. "For unto us a child is born" book
9. James' brother's "little book"
10. Prophecy by a shepherd of Tekoa
11. Foretells Jesus' birthplace
13. Description of the "armor of God"
16. NT reference to priest Melchizedek
17. Saul's conversion
18. Prophetess Deborah's story
20. David and Goliath's duel: 1st _____
22. Mother-in-law Naomi's story
23. Prophet marries prostitute
25. Death of Moses (abbr.)
26. Queen of Sheba's 1st mention: 1st _____
28. Valley of dry bones revived
29. Jeremiah's lament (abbr.)

DOWN

2. Parting of the Red Sea
4. Shortest book in the OT
5. The Magi visit Jesus
8. Balaam and the talking donkey
9. Nineveh repents
12. Contains weddings' "love" chapter: 1st _____ (abbr.)
14. King David's songbook
15. Jewish orphan becomes queen
18. Rahab's story
19. Building of Noah's ark
21. Birth of John the Baptist
24. Solomon's adage collection
25. The handwriting's on the wall!
27. Pethuel's son prophesies about an army of locusts

Answers are in the back of the book.

153

Decode the Quote

Don't wear a fake mustashe in Alabama on Sunday mornings! It is illegal to wear a fake mustashe that causes laughter in church.

Fill-in the words that match their definitions. Then, complete the solution by placing each letter that corresponds with its matching number into the spaces below. When you're finished, you'll find what BENJAMIN RUSH, Founding Father and signer of the Declaration of Independence had to say about the gospel.

Baby goose

___	___	___	___	___	___	___
4	5	6	8	14	17	4

Vacillate

___	___	___	___	___
16	21	19	3	13

Administration of the law

___	___	___	___	___	___	___
10	11	6	1	14	12	3

Heavenly instrument

2	21	13	7

Roughage

9	14	15	3	13

24 hours

18	21	20

1	2	3		4	5	6	7	3	8		5	9		10	3	6	11	6	
12	2	13	14	6	1		7	13	3	6	12	13	14	15	3	6		1	2	3
16	14	6	3	6	1		13	11	8	3	6		9	5	13		10	11	6	1
12	5	17	18	11	12	1		14	17		3	19	3	13	20				
6	14	1	11	21	1	14	5	17		5	9		8	14	9	3			

Answers are in the back of the book.

Strong Words Word Search

Find the reading's **bolded** words in the word search puzzle.

Who **among us** has never wished to have no **weaknesses**? No more **misspoken** words, hurtful remarks, mean-spirited thoughts, **embarrassing** gaffs, lost tempers, **wrongful** actions, or foolish **decisions**! Despite our **lofty ideals**, however, **each one** of us is forced to face the fact that we're far from **perfect**. Personal **shortcomings**, no matter how hard we try to avoid them, continue to play a part in our lives and in the lives of **everyone** else.

Our weaknesses never **please God**; nonetheless, He **turns them** around and uses them for **our good**. How could we ever receive His gift of a **humble heart**, except by fully **admitting** that we have **plenty to** be humble about? All we **need to do** is review what we have done and what we have **failed** to do. Why would we place **any value** on **forgive-ness** if we thought we **didn't need it**? And if we didn't need forgiveness, we'd have little **incentive** to extend it to others. Without weaknesses to **overcome**, self-mastery would **elude us**. We'd never know the **satisfaction** of having overcome a weakness, nor would we have the ability **to help** others do so, too.

Most **importantly**, our weaknesses **invite us** to draw closer to God. He has the **power** and the **desire** to **transform** our personal weaknesses into God-given **strengths**.

```
I K Q S A N Y V A L U E O E V I T N E C N I
K G B U I M P O R T A N T L Y C Z H Q F W G
N L U L S Y M P O K B B L K D W W M R E E F
A I E O B M C A H E N O I T C A F S I T A S
D Z R F E D W X A K T Q D W H S G N E X K B
M V I T U E N O H C A E D H T W A V Q P N D
I Q S Y X A P O W E R J E R N W E T T K E E
T Y E I S Q M R Y F I L E E V R N O C C S L
T N D D H T M Z O Y U N E O Y M H F I O S B
I M Q E O M R Y X D G D J O N E Y S C V E H
N T B A R I X A E T T H N V L M I Y E E S V
G U U L T S W U H O L E I P T O V W O R S L
Y R S S C S S S D O H J O S N Y A D G C F U
Z N W G O P H O D Y R T C S S R S F K O N T
L S T W M O V S G L Y L M B N P G R B M S I
P T I F I K O J V T H F D V I N Z T E E J S
D H D F N E E J N I Q F R O I F R B R Y C S
P E E C G N T E U Y W M I S O A I D D B J E
D M E G S D L L H K R S S S E Z O V O L V N
H C N R O P I J Q O X A U H D G K D O U T E
I H T E K J P D F D R G E E E S V O G F C V
E P N P I P E S Y R N L Z S T A J C R G E I
S L D O P L N F A O B P A J C I F R U N F G
P W I O I A Z B M M V E T G F W V W O O R R
B W D A R O M A U N L B I X E C U N E R E O
H T F T H E W H I P P K K Q V F E Q I W P F
```

Answers are in the back of the book.

Christian Classics Match up

Which 20th CENTURY Christian author wrote which book? Match each author to the book he or she wrote by drawing a line connecting the two. (Note: some authors wrote more than one title on the list!)

List of Authors

1. Lloyd C. Douglas
2. Dorothy L. Sayers
3. G. Campbell Morgan
4. G. K. Chesterton
5. C. S. Lewis
6. Dietrich Bonhoeffer
7. Thomas R. Kelly
8. Oswald Chambers

List of Books

a. The Everlasting Man
b. A Testament of Devotion
c. The Mind of the Maker
d. My Utmost for His Highest
e. The Robe
f. Orthodoxy
g. The Crises of the Christ
h. The Problem of Pain
i. Life Together
j. The Screwtape Letters
k. The Cost of Discipleship

Answers are in the back of the book.

Which 5th-19th CENTURY Christian author wrote which book? Match each author to the book he or she wrote by drawing a line connecting the two.

List of Authors
1. Augustine
2. Dante Alighieri
3. Julian of Norwich
4. Thomas a Kempis
5. Teresa of Avila
6. John of the Cross
7. John Calvin
8. Blaise Pascal
9. John Bunyan
10. William Law
11. Fyodor Dostoevsky

List of Books
a. The Imitation of Christ
b. Revelations of Divine Love
c. The Brothers Karamazov
d. Divine Comedy
e. Confessions
f. The Interior Castle
g. A Serious Call to a Devout and Holy Life
h. Pensees
i. The Pilgrim's Progress
j. Dark Night of the Soul
k. Institutes of the Christian Religion

Answers are in the back of the book.

PAGE 6/7

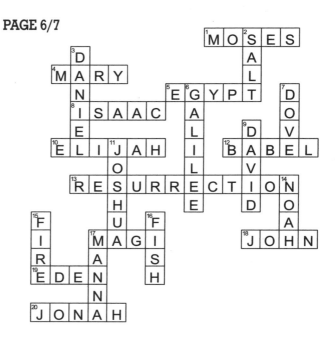

```
                          ¹M O S E S
        ³D                   A
      ⁴M A R Y               L
        N           ⁵E ⁶G Y P T        ⁷D
        ⁸I S A A C       A              O
        E               L      ⁹D       V
     ¹⁰E L I J A H ¹¹  L     ¹²B A B E L
            O          I       V
         ¹³R E S U R R E C T I O N ¹⁴
            H          E       D    O
  ¹⁵F       U     ¹⁶F                A
   I       ¹⁷M A G I                 A
   R        A      S       ¹⁸J O H N
  ¹⁹E D E N N      H
   ²⁰J O N A H
```

PAGE 8/9

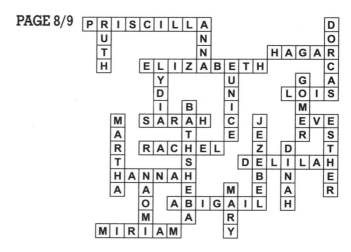

```
P R I S C I L L A                 D
R U T H         N       H A G A R O
T         E L I Z A B E T H       R
H         Y     N             G   C
          D     U          L O I S A
          I   B C          M       S
  M     S A R A H   J       E V E
  A       T   C   J E       R   S
  A   R A C H E L   Z   D       T
  R       S       D E L I L A H
  T     H A N N A H B   N       E
  H       A   E   M E   A       R
  A       O ¹⁷A B I G A I L
          M   E   R   H
  M I R I A M     Y
```

1. False. Jesus said, "I am the way, the truth, and the life: no man cometh unto the Father, but by me" (John 14:6).

2. True. "Every house is builded by some man; but he that built all things is God" (Hebrews 3:4).

3. True. "In my Father's house are many mansions: if it were not so, I would have told you. I go to prepare a place for you" (John 14:2).

4. False. "If your brother or sister sins, go and point out their fault, just between the two of you. If they listen to you, you have won them over" (Matthew 18:15 NIV).

5. False. "If you, Lord, kept a record of sins, Lord, who could stand? But with you there is forgiveness" (Psalm 130:3-4 NIV).

6. False. "Forgive, and ye shall be forgiven" (Luke 6:37).

7. False. "If ye love me, keep my commandments" (John 14:15).

8. True. "The fruit of the Spirit is love, joy, peace, forbearance, kindness, goodness, faithfulness, gentleness and self-control" (Galatians 5:22-23 NIV).

9. False. "If thine enemy hunger, feed him; if he thirst, give him drink" (Romans 12:20).

10. True. "Let the word of Christ dwell in you richly" (Colossians 3:16).

11. True. "With God nothing shall be impossible" (Luke 1:37).

ANSWERS

PAGE 11

Saying:
Two things
are bad for
the heart—
running
upstairs
and
running
down
people.

PAGE 12/13

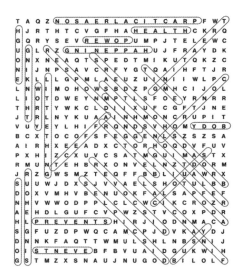

PAGE 14/15

162

PAGE 16

Possible solutions:

1. TINY
tine
vine
vane
vase
VAST

2. POOR
pool
poll
pole
pile
rile
rice
RICH

3. LESS
loss
lose
lore
MORE

4. MEAN
mead
mend
mind
KIND

5. HOLD
hole
pole
pale
pave
gave
GIVE

PAGE 17

1. D (1 Samuel 17)
2. H (Genesis 12)
3. A (Judges 4)
4. F (2 Corinthians 6)
5. I (Acts 9)
6. J (Esther 4)
7. B (Exodus 3)
8. G (Matthew 1)
9. C (Mark 1)
10. E (Jonah 1)

PAGE 18/19

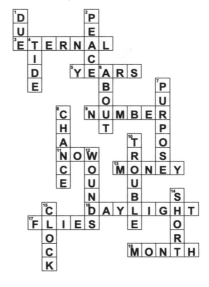

163

PAGE 20/21

S	N	I	P	S		D	A	S	H		S	L	E	D
L	A	D	E	N		I	S	L	E		B	E	M	A
O	P	E	R	A		E	T	U	I		E	V	I	L
B	E	A	S	T	S		E	G	G	S		E	L	I
		I	C	I	E	R		H	O	M	E	Y		
A	B	R	A	H	A	M			T	W	O			
B	O	O			M	O	S	E	S		A	D	A	M
E	R	M	A			T	O	T			B	E	B	E
L	E	E	R		J	E	S	U	S			A	B	S
			E	G	O			D	E	B	O	R	A	H
	I	S	A	A	C		C	E	L	L	S			
P	T	A		B	U	R	R		L	U	M	B	E	R
L	A	N	D		L	O	O	P		F	I	O	N	A
O	L	E	O		A	L	S	O		F	U	N	D	S
T	Y	R	E		R	E	S	T		S	M	A	S	H

PAGE 22/23

Answers:
dermis,
glower,
tulip,
caravan,
hobnob,
yolk

I have been driven many times to my knees by the overwhelming conviction that I had absolutely no other place to go.

PAGE 24

1. Eve's sheaves
2. Luke's dukes
3. Noah's boas
4. Ruth's booths
5. Aaron's herons
6. Mark's parks
7. Paul's stalls
8. John's fawns

PAGE 25

1. J
2. K
3. A
4. F
5. H
6. B
7. D
8. I
9. E
10. C
11. G

PAGE 26

1. A 2. C 3. B 4. C 5. B 6. A 7. B 8. C 9. B 10. A

PAGE 27

1. CARNATION 2. DAFFODIL 3. GLADIOLUS
4. SNAPDRAGON 5. PANSY 6. AZALEA
7. DAHLIA Answer: DAISIES

PAGE 28/29

PAGE 30

Answers: head, hold, box, strong

PAGE 31

1. B
2. A
3. B
4. C
5. A
6. A
7. C
8. A
9. B
10. B

PAGE 32/33

Crossword answers: MAJOR, WONDERFUL, GIVE, OUTDR..., GENEROUS, PLENTY, EXPECT, VAST, FRUIT, BOUNTY, LIVERN..., GIV..., CREAM, REAP, LARGE, CONTENT, PRAY, HARVEST, SURPRISED, HELPS, GIFT, BLESS...

PAGE 34

S	1. sheets	2. these	3. thee	S
U	4. mouse	5. some	6. ose	M
N	7. sprain	8. pairs	9. spar	I
N	10. lemon	11. mole	12. Moe	L
Y	13. teary	14. rate	15. tar	E

PAGE 35

1. Fine 2. Sole 3. Well 4. Fair 5. Bow 6. Lead 7. Ground
8. Tip 9. Desert 10. Wind 11. Rose

PAGE 36/37

PAGE 38

1. F (Matthew 14:24-25) 2. H (Luke 23:44-46) 3. B (Genesis 7:12)
4. A (Acts 2:2-4) 5. C (Exodus 10:13-20) 6. D (1 Kings 19:11-12)
7. G (Matthew 28:2-6) 8. E (Jonah 4:6-8)

PAGE 39

1. C
2. A
3. C
4. A
5. C
6. A
7. B
8. B

PAGE 40/41

O	M	A	H	A		C	O	T		A	C	P
L	A	S	E	R		R	A	H		L	Y	E
E	T	H	I	C		E	R	R		O	C	T
		S	H	O	W		O	V	U	L	E	
B	A	T	T	E	R		S	N	I	D	E	R
A	D	D		R	A	C	K	E	T			
T	O	S	S		C	U	E		A	L	I	F
		H	O	L	D	T	O		A	C	E	
K	A	R	A	T	E		C	L	A	W	E	D
N	E	I	G	H		W	H	I	R			
U	S	S		E	P	A		V	E	I	N	S
R	O	E		R	E	F		E	N	N	U	I
L	P	N		S	A	T		R	A	N	T	S

ANSWERS

167

PAGE 42

1. Think clearly
2. Research
3. Objectivity
4. Discernment
5. Root cause
6. Planning
Answer:
PRAYER

PAGE 43

1. G 2. A 3. I 4. C 5. H
6. E 7. B 8. F 9. D

PAGE 44/45

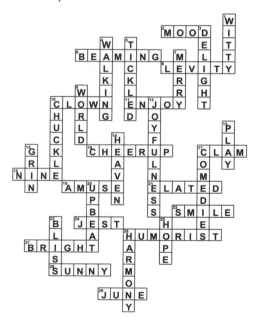

PAGE 46/47

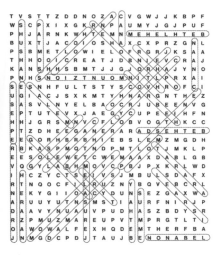

PAGE 48

Answer:
watch, coffee,
pace, Maker

PAGE 49

1. E
2. H
3. A
4. F
5. B
6. D
7. C
8. G

PAGE 50/51

ANSWERS

PAGE 52/53

1. Open	3. Burdened	5. Mate	7. Stick
Under	Do	Self	Ride
Even	Coat	Hired	Kill
HANDED	OVER	HELP	JOY
2. Place	4. Free	6. Looking	8. Belly
Time	Less	Will	Stock
One	Giver	Feel	Gas
ANY	CARE	GOOD	LAUGHING

PAGE 54/55

Answers: vote, sing, worship, buoy, malign, cod
Oh, what a happy soul I am, Although I cannot see,
I am resolved that in this world, Contented I will be.

PAGE 56

Bible verse: I am with you always, even unto the end of the world. (Matthew 28:20)

PAGE 57

1. c (Genesis 4:9),
2. a (Matthew 19:18-19),
3. b (John 19:5),
4. a (Luke 1:38)
5. c (Matthew 5:1-9),
6. b (Acts 3:6),
7. c (Esther 4:15-16)

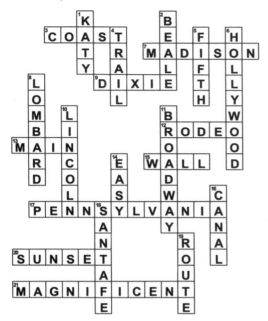

PAGE 60

Answers:
will,
news,
night,
good

PAGE 61

1. C (1 Samuel 1) 2. G (Genesis 18)
3. A (2 Corinthians 12) 4. D (Exodus 14)
5. I (Psalm 51) 6. H (Matthew 8)
7. E (1 Kings 3) 8. B (Luke 8)
9. F (Luke 15)

ANSWERS

ANSWERS

PAGE 62/63

ANSWERS

1. My thoughts are **not** your thoughts, neither are your **ways** my **ways**, saith the Lord. (Isaiah 55:8)

2. Whatsoever things are true, whatsoever things are **honest**, whatsoever things are just, whatsoever things are pure, whatsoever things are lovely, whatsoever things are of good **report**; if there be any **virtue**, and if there be **any** praise, think on these things. (Philippians 4:8)

3. I know the thoughts that I think **toward** you, saith the Lord, thoughts of peace, and not of **evil**, to **give** you an expected end. (Jeremiah 29:11)

4. The **counsel** of the Lord standeth forever, the thoughts of his heart to all **generations**. (Psalm 33:11)

5. **Which** of you with taking **thought** can add to his stature **one** cubit? (Luke 12:25)

6. A person may think their own ways are **right**, but the Lord **weighs** the heart. (Proverbs 21:2 NIV)

7. His **delight** is in the law of the Lord; and in his law doth he **meditate** day and **night**. (Psalm 1:2)

8. If you think you are standing **firm**, be **careful** that you don't **fall**! (1 Corinthians 10:12 NIV)

9. **Search** me, O God, and know my **heart**: try me, and know **my** thoughts. (Psalm 139:23)

10. **Commit** thy **works** unto the Lord, and thy thoughts shall be **established**. (Proverbs 16:3)

11. The word of God...is a **discerner** of the thoughts and **intents** of the heart. (Hebrews 4:12)

12. Jesus **knew** what they were **thinking** and asked, "Why are you thinking these **things** in your **hearts**?" (Luke 5:22 NIV)

PAGE 66/67

PAGE 68

Possible solutions:	2. FEAR	4. REAL	5. TRUE
	tear	teal	tree
	team	tell	free
1. HURT	tram	till	fret
hart	pram	tile	feet
halt	PRAY	rile	fest
hale		rife	lest
bale	3. STAY	LIFE	lost
balm	slay		lose
CALM	flay		LOVE
	fray		
	frat		
	fret		
	FREE		

PAGE 69

1. B. 2. A. 3. C. 4. C. 5. B. 6. C. 7. A. 8. C.

PAGE 70/71

1. Moses 2. Hezekiah 3. Gideon 4. Rebekah 5. Paul
6. Sarah 7. Martha 8. Jairus 9. Bartimaeus 10. Jabez
11. Thief on the cross 12. Elijah

PAGE 72/73

PAGE 74

G	1. GRASP	2. SPAR	3. RAP	S
A	4. PRAISES	5. SPIRES	6. PRESS	I
Z	7. GRAZED	8. GRADE	9. DARE	G
E	10. THINE	11. THIN	12. NIT	H
S	13. STARE	14. RATE	15. ERA	T

PAGE 75

1. D. 2. G. 3. F. 4. B. 5. E. 6. A. 7. H. 8. C.

PAGE 76

1. B. 2. B. 3. A. 4. B. 5. C. 6. A. 7. B. 8. A. 9. A. 10. C.

PAGE 77

1. TEAM BEAM 2. GRACE PLACE 3. BLISS KISS
4. SMILE STYLE 5. NEW VIEW 6. SWEET RETREAT
7. SMART HEART 8. DEVOUT SHOUT
9. FINE SHINE 10. WINK LINK

PAGE 78/79

PAGE 80/81

Answers: atlas, crinoline, jam, feud, hoopla
The doctrines of Jesus are simple, and tend
all to the happiness of man.

PAGE 82/83

¹A	²L	³L	■	⁴S	⁵E	⁶A
⁷P	O	I	■	⁸O	W	L
⁹E	B	B	■	¹⁰D	E	B
■	■	■	■	■	■	■
¹¹T	¹²W	¹³O	■	¹⁴E	¹⁵R	¹⁶A
¹⁷B	A	A	■	¹⁸G	A	P
¹⁹A	S	K	■	²⁰G	Y	P

PAGE 84

1. C. 2. E. 3. A. 4. D. 5. G. 6. F. 7. B.

PAGE 85

1. D. 2. F. 3. A. 4. C. 5. B. 6. G. 7. E.

ANSWERS

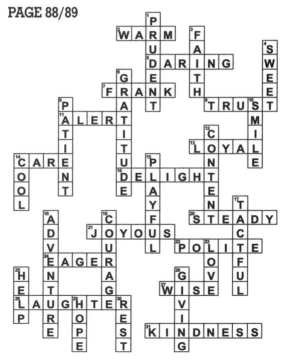

178

PAGE 90/91

Answers:
alms, young, jaded, bovine, writhe

This shall my song through eternity be, "oh, what a wonder that Jesus loves me!"

PAGE 92

Saying: Though we travel the world over to find the beautiful, we must carry it with us or we find it not.

PAGE 93

1. H.
2. D.
3. A.
4. I.
5. C.
6. E.
7. F.
8. B.
9. G.

PAGE 94/95

PAGE 96

1. Stamp collector: Philatelist
2. Ancestry seeker: Genealogist
3. Code breaker: Cryptologist
4. Coin collector: Numismatist
5. Lettering artist: Calligrapher
6. Bird observer: Ornithologist
7. Beekeeper: Apiarist
8. GPS-armed searcher: Geocacher
9. Cliff descender: Rappeller
10. Book collector: Bibliophile
11. Postcard collector: Deltiologist
12. Music enthusiast: Audiophile

PAGE 97

J	1. JOSEPH	2. HOPES	3. SHOE	P
U	4. PUREES	5. SPREE	6. REPS	E
D	7. TENSED	8. TEENS	9. SEEN	T
A	10. AWARE	11. WARE	12. RAW	E
S	13. ASSERT	14. STARE	15. SATE	R

PAGE 98/99

S H A G		E B B		S A T
C A R E		P E A		E R I E
O V E N		A D S		N A D A
F O N T S		L A I D		
F C A		P S A L M		G O T
	D R U M		P R O N E	
M E A N I E		P R O V E N	
U R B A N		C R I B		
M R S		T A L O N		T A I
	O S L O		T W I G S	
A B B R		U S S		A B E L
B U L B		L E O		V I N E
C D T		A D D		E A T S

PAGE 100

1. A
2. A
3. C
4. B
5. A
6. B
7. C

PAGE 101

1. E 2. C 3. G 4. A 5. B 6. F 7. D

PAGE 102/103

PAGE 104

1. Serenity
2. Satisfaction
3. Pleasure
4. Enjoyment
5. Fulfillment
6. Achievement
7. Insight

Answer: SUCCESS

PAGE 105

1. HARD
hart (or pard)
part
port
sort
SOFT

2. MEAN
bean
bead
bend
bind
KIND

3. HATE
pate
path
pith
PITY

4. COLD
cord
word
worm
WARM

5. PAIN
cain
coin
loin
loan
lean
dean
deal
HEAL

PAGE 106/107

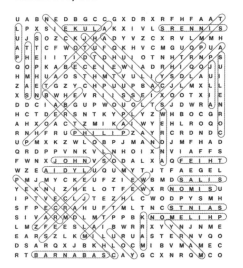

PAGE 108/109

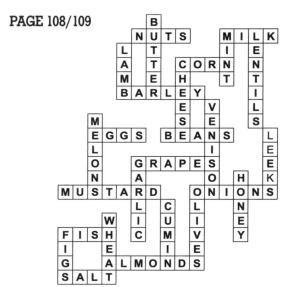

PAGE 110

1. **COMPASS**ION 2. BLES**SING** 3. PER**SEVER**ANCE 4. O**PEN**HANDED
5. AP**PROP**RIATE 6. AMI**CABLE** 7. UNPRE**TENT**IOUS
8. C**OUR**TEOUS 9. CON**SIDE**RATE 10. SUP**PORT**IVE

PAGE 111   1. C 2. F 3. I 4. G 5. B 6. D 7. A 8. E 9. H

PAGE 112/113

PAGE 114

1. Raven haven 2. Lease peace 3. Grace place or grace space
4. Higher desire 5. Found ground 6. Take break 7. Rest quest
8. Less stress 9. Draw awe 10. Feel Real

PAGE 115

1. B (Job 19:25) 2. A (Matthew 5:9) 3. B (John 1:46) 4. C (Acts
9:13) 5. A (Psalm 51:4) 6. B (Luke 2:29) 7. A (Acts 5:38-39 NIV)

PAGE 116/117

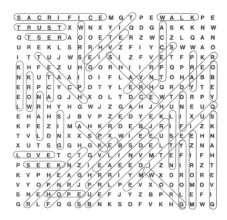

PAGE 118/119

Answers: fortune,
glum, wiggle,
halvah, taps, flood
For what avail the
plough or sail,
or land or life,
if freedom fail?

PAGE 120

1) John 3:16, 2) Psalm 139:14, 3) 1 John 4:16, 4) Zephaniah 3:17,
5) 1 Corinthians 10:31, 6) Micah 6:8, 7) 2 Corinthians 5:17

PAGE 121   Answers: bird, less, sick, love

PAGE 122/123

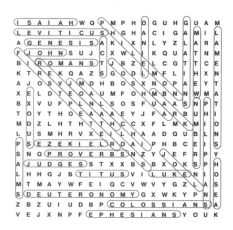

PAGE 124

Answers will vary:
eel, enliven, esteem, heel, hem, hen, hi, hit, home, honk, hoot, hot, how, howl, hunk, I, in, ink, is, it, jaw, jaws, jest, Jew, jewel, Jewish, jive, join, joist, jostle, jot, jowl, junk, just, jut, kill, kills, kiss, kisses, kin, kit, kneel, knit, lee, leek, lest, let, link, live, lit, lithe, loom, look, loose, lose, loss, lot, low, me, mesh, mess, mew, mink, mist, monk, moose, moot, moist, moss, mouse, move, mow, nil, no, noose, nose, noses, note, notes, now, on, owl, owls, onto, sank, see, seek, sees, set, sew, shot, silk, sin, sink, skill, skills, skin, skit, sleek, slew, slim, slink, slit, slot, sloth, sloths, slow, slum, smooth, so, sole, solemn, solo, solve, soot, soul, sow, stink, stool, stew, sum, sunk, sweet, swish, swoon, tee, these, thin, think, this, those, tin, took, tool, tow, tune, until, unto, vole, volume, vote, vow, we, went, west, wet, whee, wheel, whistle, whim, wish, wishes, will, wilt, wink, wit, won, wool, woven.

PAGE 125

Answer:
It is only when men begin to worship that they begin to grow.

PAGE 126/127

1-b) Cape Cod
2-b) Speedwell
3-b) Plymouth, England
4-a) 2 dogs
5-b) Separatists
6-c) Compact
7-d) all three
8-c) codfish
9-c) Wampanoag
10-b) four inches

PAGE 128/129

Answers: young, flair, steam, abode, clove, habitat
America! America! May God thy gold refine till all success be nobleness and every gain divine.

PAGE 130/131

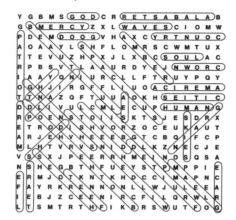

PAGE 132

Answers:
1) b, 2) b and c,
3) c, 4) a and b,
5) a, 6) c,
7) b—out of
the 66 books,
Paul wrote 14.

PAGE 133   Answers: yard, mouse, hill, church.

PAGE 134: Answers will vary

Answers: a, able, abs, ah, aha, all, alms, am, amaze, are, ash, ashes, bale, ball, balm, bam, barb, bare, base, bash, bass, bear, bell, blame, blaze, bra, brash, brass, braze, ear, earl, ha, has, hale, ham, hash, hassle, haze, hazel, he, her, heal, hear, hell, hem, herb, hill, la, lab, label, lam, lamb, lame, lash, lass, laze, lear, ma, male, mall, mar, marble, mare, marl, mars, marsh, mash, mass, maze, me, meal, mesh, mess, ram, rash, rasher, raze, real, rear, sable, sale, same, sash, sass, sea, seal, seam, sear, sell, shale, sham, shame, share, shazam, she, shea, shear, shill, slab, slash, small, zeal, zebra

PAGE 135

Answer: I cannot conceive how a man could look up into the heavens and say there is no God.

PAGE 136/137

Answer: 1) whale, 2) mask, 3) yodel, 4) harangue, 5) hilt
Make sure you are doing what God wants you to do—
then do it with all your strength.

PAGE 138/139

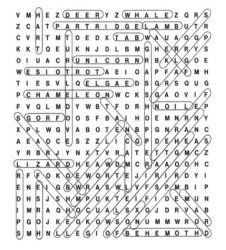

PAGE 140/141

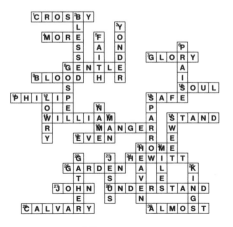

PAGE 142/143

Answers:
1) Annie Hasseltine Judson,
2) Sojourner Truth, 3) Hannah Whithall Smith, 4) Ida Scudder,
5) Hannah Adams,
6) Amanda Berry Smith,
7) Fanny Crosby, 8) Lottie Moon

PAGE 144

Answer:
That book, sir, is the rock on which our republic rests.

PAGE 145

Answers:
word,
walk,
hair,
cross

PAGE 146/147

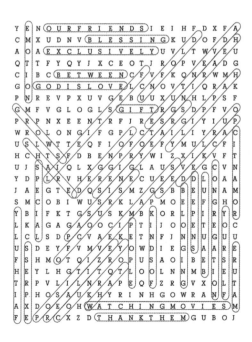

PAGE 148/149

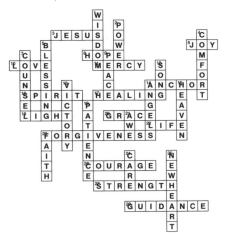

PAGE 150/151

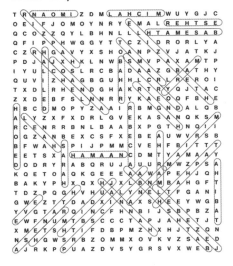

PAGE 152/153

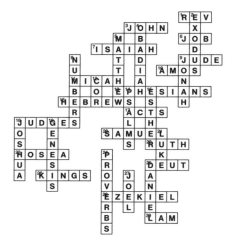

PAGE 154/155

Answers: gosling, waver, justice, harp, fiber, day.
The gospel of Jesus Christ
prescribes the wisest rules for just
conduct in every situation of life.

PAGE 156/157

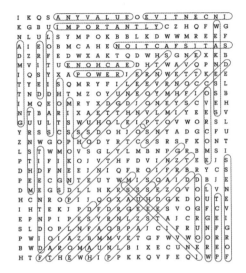

PAGE 158

1. E. 2. C. 3. G. 4. A & F 5. H & J. 6. I & K. 7. B. 8. D.

PAGE 159

1. E. 2. D. 3. B. 4. A. 5. F. 6. J. 7. K. 8. H.
9. I. 10. G 11. C.

Trust in

the LORD

with all

thine heart.

Proverbs 3:5